The
Splendid
LEADER

ISBN: 09781596-7-5

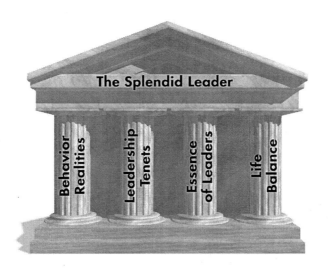

INTRODUCTION

Many books have been written to help individuals understand what great leaders do. We encourage you to read as many of these books as you can, because we truly believe that leadership, like any other subject, can be learned--it just takes study, hard work, determination, and courage. Our concept of Splendid Leadership is derived from real-world experiences combined with recognized academic theory on what it takes to become a truly Splendid Leader. This book is based upon observations and discussions with effective leaders and followers, as well as a combined 80 years of practical experience in leadership and management positions between the authors. During those 80 years, we looked up the organizational ladder at leaders, looked sideways at peer leaders as they climbed the ladder, and eventually, rose to levels where we could look down the ladder at other leaders who were still climbing. All of these observations contributed to our understanding and learning about the art of leadership. This book, therefore, contains a framework as well as practical examples of what you can do to become a Splendid Leader and how you can help populate your organization with **Splendid Leaders--Everywhere!**

The Splendid Leadership framework consists of four pillars: (1) Behavior Realities; (2) Leadership Tenets; (3) Essence of Leaders; and (4) Life Balance. We believe Splendid Leaders understand and apply the concepts of each pillar in their professional and personal lives. Furthermore, we are convinced people learn most effectively by hearing or reading stories. Therefore, we present real-life stories that illustrate how Splendid Leaders practice the concepts of each pillar. We hope, as you read these stories, you can relate the Splendid Leader concepts to your own experiences--in your workplace, your community, and your personal life. And more importantly, we trust this book will spur you along the journey to Splendid Leadership.

Authors' Note: Occasionally, we will insert personal comments like this: *When trying to find the right word to describe the type of leader we wanted to illustrate in this book, we came upon the word* **splendid**, *a somewhat old-fashioned adjective that means: "fine, grand, superb, impressive, marvelous, wonderful, fabulous, and super." Wouldn't you want to be or want to follow such a leader?*

CONTENTS

ACKNOWLEDGEMENTS

He who influences the thought of his times;
Influences the times that follow.

— Elbert Hubbard

In writing this book, the journey has been as important as the destination. We have been reminded over and over again of the tremendous people who surround us. These people have generously and eagerly provided support, encouragement, constructive criticism, and an undying commitment to help capture our thoughts in this book. Although the list of these people is long, we would like to specifically express our appreciation to the following few for their contributions:

Diane Phillips	Editing and Valuable Suggestions
Lisa Boone-Berry	Editing and a Fresh Viewpoint
Keith Cole	Sounding Board, Network Connections, and Unique Ideas
Samantha Barnett	Creative Artwork
Andrew Gilmore	Publishing Expertise
John Hart	Professional Advice

We would be remiss if we did not thank our friends who so graciously agreed to allow us to share their stories and examples in this book. Our spouses, Fran and Lloyd, were incredibly understanding and supportive throughout the entire journey. Also, our children never stopped believing in us and pushing us to "get it done!" Finally, thanks to all the tremendous leaders from whom we learned and who served as models for our concept of *The Splendid Leader*.

Chapter 1.1

Why We Do What We Do

Understanding Behavior

"We need people who can dream of things that never were."

— John F. Kennedy

The following paraphrased quote by Dwight D. Eisenhower, provides the basis for understanding why **Behavior Realities** is a key pillar of Splendid Leadership: "Leadership is the art of getting people to do something that needs to be done because they want to do it." If you want to inspire people to do what needs to be done, you need to understand why people do what they do.

It is extremely important for Splendid Leaders to understand Behavior Realities because they affect how people will respond to leadership, as well as why people behave as they do in their work and daily environments. In other words, one can become a more effective leader by understanding and leveraging Behavior Realities to achieve desired behaviors, and thereby getting the right things done.

According to Steve Cato at the Federal Executive Institute, there are three categories of Behavior Realities: historical, current, and anticipatory (Cato). Examples of the first category of behavior "influencers," Historical Realities, are listed in Figure 1.1.0. Many of these Historical Realities are factors that are set early in our lives. While these ingrained factors certainly do influence behavior, leaders have a limited ability to affect these factors in others. For example, leaders cannot change an employee's cultural background nor their developmental environment. We should, however, be aware of Historical Realities because they can influence responses to leadership.

Historical Realities		
Heredity		
Cultural Background		
Socialization		
Environment		
Education		
Training		
Personality		
Values		
Morals		

Figure 1.1.0

The second category is Current Realities, which includes factors such as those listed in Figure 1.1.1. These factors are often identified as influencing employee behavior in the workplace. For example, leaders should seek ways to satisfy employees' needs for recognition of their accomplishments and contributions. While these factors cannot be ignored, we do not believe they are the dominant reasons for behavior, nor should they be the main focus of Splendid Leaders.

Historical Realities	Current Realities	
Heredity	Personal Gain	
Cultural Background	Peer Pressure	
Socialization	Hierarchy of Needs	
Environment	Recognition	
Education	Loyalty	
Training	Expectations	
Personality	Curiosity	
Values	Habit	
Morals	Contribution	

Figure 1.1.1

Examples of the third category, Anticipatory Realities, are listed in Figure 1.1.2. Anticipatory Realities touch the hearts of people--they are truly at the core of what motivates people's behavior. Anticipatory Realities can make monumental changes in the world, as evidenced by incredible feats accomplished in support of dreams, visions, and utopian ideas!

Historical Realities	Current Realities	Anticipatory Realities
Heredity	Personal Gain	Dreams
Cultural Background	Peer Pressure	Visions
Socialization	Hierarchy of Needs	Utopian Ideas
Environment	Recognition	
Education	Loyalty	
Training	Expectations	
Personality	Curiosity	
Values	Habit	
Morals	Contribution	

Figure 1.1.2

We like to ask individuals or groups: "Why do you behave the way you do, and what *most* motivates you to do the things you do each day?" Responses to this question are fairly predictable because most individuals easily identify with Historical and Current Realities (where they've been and where they are). But surprisingly, answers that fit into the third category, Anticipatory Realities, are rarely provided!

> *We attribute the lack of Anticipatory Reality responses to the fact that they can be embarrassing or revealing, and therefore risky to share. When was the last time you shared your dreams with someone?*

When thinking about all the **Behavior Realities** simultaneously, the most important part of understanding behavior is this: <u>**Anticipatory Realities far outweigh the sum of Historical Realities plus Current Realities**</u> in explaining why people behave the way the do. In other words, Anticipatory Realities are many times more causal in influencing behavior!

If you look at some of the most notable leaders in history, you'll recognize that they understood the power of Anticipatory Realities. Take for instance:

— Dr. Martin Luther King Jr.'s famous speech, "I have a dream that my four little children will one day live in a nation where they will not be judged by the color of their skin but by the content of their character. I have a dream today!"

> *What response do you think he would have received if he had said, "I have a strategic plan"?*

— President John F. Kennedy's phrase, "Ask not what your country can do for you; ask what you can do for your country!"

> *What response do you think he would have received if he had said, "Everyone be a volunteer"?*

Or, what about his bold statement, "We choose to go to the moon. We choose to go to the moon in this decade and do . . . other things not because they are easy but because they are hard." (And this was stated even though the technology to do so was not yet proven!)

> *What if he had said, "Let's invest in scientific research"?*

— Winston Churchill's statement, "We shall defend our island, whatever the cost may be, we shall fight on the beaches, we shall fight on the landing grounds, we shall fight in the fields and in the streets, we shall fight in the hills; we shall never surrender."

> *What if he had said, "Let's fight until we win this war"?*

— Franklin D. Roosevelt's statement, "The only thing we have to fear is fear itself--nameless, unreasoning, unjustified terror which paralyzes needed efforts to convert retreat into advance."

What if he had just said, "Don't be afraid"?

— President Ronald Reagan's famous "Berlin Wall" speech, "General Secretary Gorbachev, if you seek peace, if you seek prosperity for the Soviet Union and Eastern Europe, if you seek liberalization: Come here to this gate! Mr. Gorbachev, open this gate! Mr. Gorbachev, tear down this wall!"

Would he have gotten the same response had he said, "Gorby, this wall has got to go"?

There is an undeniable link between understanding the power of Anticipatory Realities and the ability to be a Splendid Leader. Words that touch the heart can be incredibly influential when desiring to impact the behavior of others.

Of course there are also examples in history when negative behavior was inspired by Anticipatory Realities--but we prefer to focus on the positive.

In the workplace, the ability to affect the behavior of others through Anticipatory Realities is critical. But, *how* do you tap into the power of Anticipatory Realities in the workplace and in your personal life? In the following chapters, we will describe techniques and provide examples that can be used by leaders to reap the benefits of understanding Anticipatory Realities.

Chapter 1.2

Why We Do What We Do

The Impact of Vision Statements and BHAGs

"Go confidently in the direction of your dreams,
live the life you have imagined."
— Henry David Thoreau

Collins and Porras wrote that visionary companies use "Big Hairy Audacious Goals (BHAGs)" as a powerful way to stimulate progress.

> A true BHAG is clear and compelling, serves as a unifying focal point of effort, and acts as a catalyst for team spirit. It has a clear finish line, so the organization can know when it has achieved the goal; people like to shoot for finish lines. A BHAG engages people--it reaches out and grabs them. It is tangible, energizing, and highly focused. People get it right away; it takes little or no explanation (Collins and Porras 73).

Vision statements and BHAGs are Anticipatory Realities. You can use either an organizational BHAG or a well-crafted vision statement as a method to unify and inspire all the hearts in the workplace.

And, you can create a personal BHAG to touch *your own* heart. Organizational and personal Anticipatory Realities have the end result of influencing behaviors in order to turn those visions and BHAGs into realities.

Organizational Visions

Because vision statements are such an important tool for Splendid Leaders, here are some thoughts on what constitutes a good one:

1. First and foremost, it should be short--ideally only a few words. The appeal of brevity is obvious. All employees can easily remember a brief statement, and therefore, they are more likely to repeat it. Frequent repetition keeps it in the forefront of all activities and enhances the likelihood of achieving the vision.

2. The vision statement should be action-oriented, painting a word picture. An example of a short, action-oriented vision statement is "Crush Adidas," a Nike Corporation internal vision from the 1960s (Collins and Porras 72). It fits the first two principles for a good vision statement. Not only is it short, but the word *crush* conveys action, intensity, and a no-nonsense attitude. You can almost *hear* the vision statement. And, directly identifying your competition in the vision statement can certainly focus employees' attention!

3. If possible, a good vision statement should be lyrical. It should easily roll off the tongue and be melodic--like the former General Electric statement, "We bring good things to life." Another example of a good lyrical vision statement is McDonald's, "You deserve a break today."

> *Did you "hear" the music in your mind when you read these statements?*

4. A good vision statement should project a future state. A great example of this concept is the vision statement for the Aeronautical Systems Center (ASC), a U.S. Air Force unit in Dayton, Ohio: "The Birthplace, Home, and Future of Aerospace." Note, this vision covers the entire time-spectrum for aerospace: from native sons, Orville and Wilbur Wright's invention of the airplane; to the development of today's airplanes; to the idea that the future of the entire aerospace community rests in the hands of ASC employees--pretty heady stuff!

> *OK, we were part of the team that helped develop this vision statement, so please excuse us if our pride is showing.*

5. Some of the best vision statements we have encountered do a great job of capturing the heart of each employee on a *personal* level. The U.S. Army's former statement, "Be all you can be," is an excellent example. It conveyed that anyone who joined the Army could achieve his or her full potential while simultaneously accomplishing the Army's mission. Thus, every member of the Army was encouraged to be his or her best in the service of our nation's defense.

> *Vision statements can change with time to meet target audiences, such as "An Army of One" (2001-2006) and "Army Strong" (2006-present).*

Another statement that captures the heart is the Pfizer Pharmaceutical's vision, "Life is our life's work." Wouldn't you want to work for a company whose main focus is to improve the quality of everyone's life?

Now, with all these good thoughts on what makes an effective vision statement, how do you go about creating one for your organization that is truly an Anticipatory Reality? Well, it's not easy! Organizations often invest a considerable amount of time, energy, and money into creating vision statements to inspire their workforce. We believe the most important characteristic of a corporate vision statement is that it be truly communal. How a vision statement is developed can have a tremendous effect on how well it is "invested in and owned by" the people of the organization. Inclusiveness engenders a commitment to make the vision a reality. As we said, there is no easy way to develop the best vision statement for your organization, but we suggest the following steps as a way to start:

1. Actively involve a broad cross section of your organization in the development of the vision statement by seeking their inputs and incorporating their feedback. Do not limit the development team to just the top of the organizational management structure. Remember, great ideas can reside at all levels in the organization. A broad cross section will ensure a wide variety of input is obtained, and it will ultimately help in the dissemination of the selected vision statement. This approach also reinforces the concept of ownership. But whatever you do, do not just make it your vision--make it the *organization's* vision.

2. Try out the various vision statement options on other members of your extended organization--on your customers, on your retired employees, even on your neighbors. If you have to explain what the vision statement means, then it is time to go back to the drawing board.

3. Once you have a statement that the developers are comfortable with, having it fully embraced by the organization may be an even bigger challenge. There is no magic formula; it is a matter of communication, communication, and more communication. All organizations have "mavens," trusted people at various levels in the organization who are convincingly vocal and have the ears of others in the workforce. Target and enlist your organizational mavens to help embed, embrace, and communicate your organization's vision. Have a roll-out ceremony, utilize group meetings, send notices and e-mails, put it on posters, and do anything else you can think of to emphasize and reinforce the vision!

AN ORGANIZATIONAL VISION--THE MARCHING PATRIOTS

When asked about his most challenging leadership position, with tongue-in-cheek, Vince responds, "the President of the Carroll High School Marching Patriots Band Parents' Association!"

In his book, *The Sky Is Not the Limit*, Bart Barthelemy writes about this band and its vision to become the national champion of marching bands for like-sized schools. Barthelemy explains the incredible work band director, Dave Luzio, and approximately 135 students did to pursue this goal (Barthelemy 30-32). Behind the scenes, were the parents who provided financial and logistical support. For three years, Vince and his wife, Fran, served as co-presidents of the parents' organization. According to Vince, this was one of his most challenging leadership jobs because nearly every parent knew the right answers to whatever problems the group faced, and of course, nearly all the solutions were different! The challenge was to build consensus in this all-volunteer organization.

One technique, which worked well in this situation, was to continually remind the group of the all-important vision--winning a national championship. This unifying vision motivated amazing feats. They overcame incredible barriers because they believed, along with the band director and the students, that the goal could be achieved, even by a small, private high school. It was clear that the "underdog" factor became a major motivator not only for the students, but also for the parents. They all felt that if they worked hard enough, they would obtain the national championship. In early 1983, the Carroll High School Marching Patriots were named the number one marching band for their school size in a national competition!

Personal BHAGs

Because a personal BHAG can be an extremely effective self-motivation technique, we encourage people to set their own BHAGs, and to think big. Don't say you want to be a lawyer; say you want to sit on the Supreme Court! Don't say you want to be a teacher; say you want to be the national teacher of the year! Don't say you want to be a pilot; say you want to fly a ship to Mars! We site these examples to encourage you to think *big*. After all, the first word in BHAG is *big*.

Still, experience shows that people are reluctant to talk openly about their Anticipatory Realities; so, one way to "break the ice" is to share your BHAG. This can also be a method of showing personal vul-nerability. What is more intimidating for a leader than sharing personal wishes, dreams, or possibilities with those who possess the ability to judge them? Leadership takes courage--sharing a personal BHAG demonstrates this quality. We have done this several times, and we are always amazed at the positive feedback we received. We have found that when putting voice to your dreams, others respond supportively. At least you will get them thinking more about it, and you may even get them to share their BHAGs. So give it a try, and talk about what you embrace as your personal BHAG--you may be pleasantly surprised by the results.

> *Now it's time to put our money where our mouths are. Here are our personal BHAGs: Vince wants to be the science advisor to the President of the United States! Donna wants to create a one-of-a-kind retreat for leaders so they can reenergize themselves and their organizations!*

Chapter 1.3

Why We Do What We Do

Effective Leaders and Efficient Managers

"Management is efficiency in climbing the ladder of success;
Leadership determines whether the ladder is leaning
against the right wall."
— Stephen R. Covey

We believe effective leaders are those who understand the power of Anticipatory Realities and know how to use it to touch hearts to achieve desired results. Efficient managers are those who possess the ability to plan, direct, manage, and control activities to achieve desired results. It is the ability to influence people's behavior through dreams, visions, and utopian ideas that distinguishes effective leaders from efficient managers. This difference is captured by: **"Leadership is by the heart, and management is by the head--and we need some of both."**

Understanding this critical difference between leadership and management enhances one's journey toward becoming a Splendid Leader. We are not suggesting you should change your focus to only Anticipatory Realities. What we are encouraging is that you find the right balance between effective leadership and efficient management by using your heart as well as your head. Not only is this balance important in individual actions; it is equally important in organizational actions.

The different behaviors between leaders and managers are manifested by their actions. We characterize these differences between leaders and managers as shown in Figure 1.3.1 (Russo). First, let's examine the Management column.

Management (Head)	
Looks for Evidence	
Weighs Facts	
Looks for Purpose	
Believes	
Seeks Satisfaction	
Thinks	

Figure 1.3.1

Many who view these management characteristics believe these actions are very important--and they are right! Every organization needs good managers.

Now, with the Leadership column added in Figure 1.3.2, read the chart horizontally; e.g., while managers look for evidence, leaders look for passion; while managers weigh facts, leaders act on faith; and so forth.

Management (Head)	Leadership (Heart)
Looks for Evidence	Looks for Passion
Weighs Facts	Acts on Faith
Looks for Purpose	Seeks Meaning
Believes	Trusts
Seeks Satisfaction	Seeks Utopia
Thinks	Dreams

Figure 1.3.2

Again, the point is that personal and organizational balance between management and leadership is critical to success. Our experiences, however, underscore the belief that Splendid Leaders make more effective use of their hearts when making most decisions.

To reiterate, one of the most important skills of a Splendid Leader is the ability to touch people's hearts. The power of the heart is a well-studied and documented concept. For example, authors who believe in the power of the heart in leadership, as documented in their books, include: *Leading from the Heart* by Jack Kahl; *The Heart Aroused* by David Whyte; *Encouraging the Heart* by Jim Kouses and Barry Posner; *Leading with the Heart* by Mike Krzyzewski; and *Primal Leadership* by Daniel Goleman, Richard Boyatzis, and Annie McKee.

Chapter 2.1

The Laws of Leadership

Start with the Heart

"Leadership is the art of getting extraordinary performance
from ordinary people."
— Anonymous

The shelves of many bookstores are overflowing with theory, advice, and experiences on leadership. Between the two of us, we have read a good sampling of this plethora, and we have come to the conclusion that there are a precious few tenets that represent what those authors have captured in various forms. In this pillar, we discuss the six leadership tenets that our experiences have taught us represent what Splendid Leaders do: Start with the Heart; Creat Trust; Equip People to Excel; Use the Word Why; Have Fun!; and Cast a Splendid Shadow.

We often use the term laws when explaining these tenets because they are universally applicable in all leadership situations. Independent of where one resides in the organizational pyramid, these laws are relevant, although their degree of applicability may vary by position within the organization. These tenets constitute a key pillar for Splendid Leaders, and we encourage you to use them in your daily leadership activities.

Start with the Heart
Create Trust
Equip People to Excel
Use the Word Why
Have Fun!
Cast a Splendid Shadow

In the next few chapters, we discuss and provide examples for how to implement the six leadership tenets. With this framework, let's "Start with the Heart."

"Find the heart of an organization,
and you have the key to unlock unparalleled performance
for the organization and all who serve it."
— *Donna J. Back*

Splendid Leaders find many ways to Start with the Heart. We have already discussed one such way--the use of Anticipatory Realities. There are many others including mentoring, investing in training, expressing care and concern over non-job-related difficulties, verbal expressions of appreciation, assigning challenging projects, displaying confidence in an employee's ability to exceed expectations, and tending to the health and safety of employees. In this chapter, we will cover two additional ways: recognition and communication.

Appropriately rewarding people has always been an important element of a leader's ability to touch employees' hearts. Unfortunately, most organizations do not have the means to provide large financial rewards to all deserving employees. Experience suggests that unless financial rewards are large enough to significantly change a person's lifestyle, they have only a marginal effect on inspiring desired behaviors. In fact, if financial rewards are very modest or if they are equally spread across many employees, they may not have a positive impact on behavior at all. Thus, leaders constantly look for other, nonfinancial ways to reward people for outstanding performance.

The Power of Naming (Recognition)

We found that awards and other tangible items named in honor of individuals have multiple benefits. "Named" awards touch the hearts of many: the people who established the award; the person honored by the naming; and the eventual recipient(s) of the named award. Likewise, naming tangible items such as buildings, conference rooms, significant days of the year, events, trophies, plazas, and gathering areas have a corresponding effect of touching the heart. The opportunities to Start with the Heart by naming are endless.

THE RUSSO SCIENCE LABORATORY

A math and science learning laboratory, the Russo Science Lab, was named in honor of Vince's efforts to inspire young students to pursue technical careers. Needless to say, Vince's heart was touched by this naming, and it certainly resulted in increasing his motivation and dedication to continue to do more and more for this K--12 outreach program. Yes, the recognition was important to him, but it was also important to those responsible for the naming since their hearts were likewise touched. Ms. Kathy Schweinfurth, manager of the K-12 outreach program, and her team placed above the entry to the laboratory a plaque that reads, "Russo Science Lab--Where Having Fun is #1." When asked why she and her team wanted to name the lab after Vince, she said, "There are really three reasons why we did it. First, when visitors come to our laboratory, it gives us a chance to tell the story about Vince and the wonderful influence he had on our endeavor. Second, it motivates us to carry on his tradition of passion and dedication to K-12 math and science education. And third, it reminds us on a daily basis of the workforce attitude that we want in our organization--one that has the same passion and dedication that Vince exhibits, and one where there is fun in the workplace!" It is clear from Kathy's comments that all of the individuals involved in the outreach program benefited by the naming.

As previously noted, the opportunities for naming are endless. The importance of this leadership tool is obvious. Now, all you have to do is institute some naming within your organization to reap the benefits.

Organizational Fellows Awards (Recognition)

Most national and international technical societies have a Fellows Program. Fellows usually represent the absolute cream-of-the-crop of the membership of the society. Often, the strictly limited number elected each year are recognized with elaborate induction ceremonies. The elected Fellows are role models with special privileges provided by the society. So, if it works so well for technical societies to inspire the entire society's membership, then a similar concept could work equally well in your workplace. Therefore, consider creating your organization's equivalent to a Fellows Program. A highly qualified and respected committee could select your organizational "Fellows," and the special privileges provided to the Fellows should be well understood by all employees. Have a unique event to announce the recipients, put their names and pictures in a prominent place and make sure their families know about the honor. We believe you will find the dual benefits are evident--the recipients will be energized and the awarding organization will be delighted.

> *We've seen this work effectively in high-tech organizations where employees are highly motivated by the desire to achieve the nonmonetary recognition as a Fellow of a nationally recognized organization. In addition, we have also seen that establishing similar awards work in nontechnical fields for secretaries, financial managers, administrative assistants, and program or account managers in a "local environment."*

What is Going On (WIGO)? (Communication)

How many times have you heard that leadership is about communication, communication, and more communication? Well, there are many ways to communicate, and you can never over communicate with the workforce. One of the best techniques we have seen is the WIGO e-mail. A good friend of ours, Dick Reynolds, used this technique very effectively. Dick wanted to make sure *everyone* (about 12,000 people) in his organization heard directly from him on subjects of importance in the workplace. He frequently held "all hands" meetings and "break room" gatherings for small groups and encouraged open personal communication via e-mails. But by far, the most effective and far-reaching communication tool was the WIGO e-mail.

Every Sunday night, Dick constructed an e-mail that discussed everything he thought was important for his people to know for the coming week.

We said he constructed the e-mail. Yes, he had some help, but there was no question that it was his e-mail.

The e-mail contained a myriad of issues: organizational, national, customer, and personnel. It was sent to every employee in the organization. Every Monday morning, the entire workforce received this e-mail and began their week with an understanding of what the boss saw as key issues regarding the organization's mission. Over time, nearly everyone looked forward to Dick's weekly e-mail. Obviously, with an organization of this size, it would be impossible for the leader to speak personally with everyone. However, the WIGO introduced a closeness to the leader that made everyone *feel* as though they had had a personal conversation with the boss. The WIGO is an efficient use of today's technology to get important messages to the workforce in a personal way that starts with the heart.

The Simple Written Note (Communication)

Although we just told you about the success of the WIGO e-mail and the power of using today's technology, we are also strong believers in the power of an older communication tool--the handwritten note. Granted, handwritten notes can be a time-consuming activity, but we have seen the strength of this means of communication many times over. Often, a simple written thank you or congratulatory note is highly valued by employees because it is clear the leader took extra time to handwrite the note, adding his or her personal touch. We have seen notes like these attached to cubical walls or in other highly visible places in an employee's work environment. The notes need not be long, but should be written on distinctive paper--brightly colored or specially bordered paper to make the note immediately recognizable as coming from the leader. Employees highly value these simple, handwritten notes because they touch the heart!

> *Now remember, we are talking about the leader writing the note in his or her own handwriting, not something drafted by a staff person and signed by the leader. While a drafted /signed note can be useful, it is much less effective than a personal note. Splendid Leaders write innumerable personal notes.*

A SIMPLE NOTE

Sometimes, the importance of these notes extends beyond the employee's heart to the hearts of their family. When one of Donna's employees passed away, the family collected mementos that had significance to the deceased and his family and displayed them at the funeral home visitation. One such memento was a handwritten note from Donna extolling the significance of the deceased employee's contribution to the organization. The note was several years old, and yet it still retained enough impact on the family to be shared during this most revered family time. Never underestimate the influence of a simple, handwritten note.

When you Start with the Heart, the rest of the Leadership Tenets just seem to fall into place. Touching the hearts of individuals provides a strong foundation that allows Splendid Leaders to continue to build an organization where people clamor to come to work and where performance continues to trump the competition.

Chapter 2.2

The Laws of Leadership

Create Trust

"How important is trust in the workplace?
If leaders can't create, restore, and sustain trust,
they might as well send everyone home."
— *Donna J. Back*

As exemplified by headlines about corporate corruptions, personal misbehaviors, and organizational failings, trust has become a scarce commodity in some of our corporate, financial, religious, political, entertainment, and sports institutions. Some go so far as to say that we have a crisis of trust.

Splendid Leaders create trust in the workplace. When trust exists in an organization, people get excited about what they do, collaboration and sharing ideas becomes the norm, channels of communication open up, and people are not afraid to make mistakes. Trust is reciprocal: you have to give it to get it, and it is built over time. Trust begets trust (Reina 23-25).

We have identified the following six elements that help leaders create trust in the workplace:

Value Contributions

Possess Competency

Constancy of Purpose

Reciprocal Support

Create Safe Zones

Keep Promises

Value Contributions

Brother Raymond Fitz, the Fr. William Ferree Professor of Social Justice at the University of Dayton, believes the first element of building trust involves seeking and respecting inputs from those who will be affected by a decision, *before the decision is made* (Fitz). He states that actively seeking out various opinions before making a decision conveys to individuals a belief the leader truly cares about them, and it assures them the leader is respectful of their thoughts and feelings. Even though a leader may make a decision that is counter to the input received from an individual, a foundation of trust is nurtured by the mere act of asking for opinions. In the press of daily decision-making, this may be viewed as a time-consuming step that could be eliminated; however, the benefit reaped in terms of establishing trust in the workplace and engendering acceptance of the decision cannot be overlooked. We refer to this as *valuing the contributions* of others.

One technique we have found effective in gathering input before a decision is rendered involves the use of *thumbs*. When decision options are being formulated, it is helpful to ask people to express their sentiments by showing a thumb up, a thumb horizontal, or a thumb down. A thumb up should mean the option is highly preferred and will be fully supported. A thumb horizontal means the individual is neutral on the option--furthermore, it means if the option is chosen, the individual with the horizontal thumb will support the option, will not speak badly of the decision, and will not seek ways to undermine the decision. When a thumb is down, that usually means the individual has real problems with the option, and if the option were chosen, he or she would have difficulty supporting it. With a thumb down response, the leader must take the extra time needed to fully understand the reason for the negative reaction. It should be noted that the use of thumbs is *not a vote* where the majority rules. Rather, it is a technique to ensure a leader is seeking inputs from those affected by the decision, and thereby, contributing to creating trust.

A word of caution is warranted at this point. With an ever-expanding global environment, make sure the thumbs approach is not offensive to the culture of the input providers.

Possess Competency

Brother Ray further states that individuals must believe their leader is *competent to make the right decision* (Fitz). This element of building trust is one that is not easily established, especially in institutions that believe "a leader is a leader" and, therefore, they can lead any organization. Our experiences have shown that when a leader possesses competency in the subject matter of the organization, building trust is much easier than in organizations where a person without the requisite competencies is put in a leadership position. Accepting the leader's competency can be subjective and filled with emotion. But, it can also be filled with genuine concern caused by the inappropriate placement of people in leadership positions for which they may not have all the requisite competencies. Splendid Leaders choose individuals who are competent in the subject matters of the organization in which they are asked to lead.

Constancy of Purpose

This element of building trust is captured with the following idea: when decisions are made, they are reasonably consistent based upon historical evidence. This means that individuals can expect a leader's decision will not be a radical departure from similar past decisions. This engenders trust by allowing employees to feel secure, confident, and comfortable with the decision. By constancy of purpose, we do not mean leaders always make totally predictable decisions.

Reciprocal Support

Trust is built when individuals subordinate their differing perspectives for the good of the enterprise. After the decision-making process is complete, reciprocal support involves employees embracing the final decision and the leader creating an environment that allows modification to the decision if conditions change.

The opposite of reciprocal support, and a sure way to damage trust, is undermining. Undermining occurs by "bad mouthing" a leader's actions or decisions, by saying a decision is supported but acting in a nonsupportive manner, or by purposefully enlisting others in an attempt to counter the leader's decision. Undermining inhibits the building of trusting relationships.

Create Safe Zones

An important technique to help build trust in organizations is to define boundaries for decision making by subordinates and to make it clear that the leader will support the subordinate's decisions within these boundaries. Even if the leader would have made a different decision, as long as the subordinate stayed within the defined boundaries or *safe zone*, the leader should support the subordinate's decision. This mechanism allows leaders to create opportunities for employees to practice leadership while at the same time, contributing to sustaining trust.

Keep Promises

Your word must be your pledge! Leaders who follow through on their commitments provide a solid foundation for building trust within organizations. When leaders keep their promises, it reinforces a trusting relationship between leaders and followers. Keeping promises becomes an organizational practice demonstrated at all levels--by leaders, managers, employees, suppliers, and customers. Need we say more?

Chapter 2.3

The Laws of Leadership

Equip People to Excel

"Count success by not how high you climb,
but, by how many you take along."
— *Will Rose*

This Leadership Tenet embodies a key raison d'être for Splendid Leaders--equipping others to achieve the vision and mission of the organization as well as developing their individual potential. It involves providing resources; equipment; time; mentoring, coaching, and networking; and education and training for success of the organization and the individual. Equipping others allows the workforce to accomplish not only the task at hand, but also to grow as individuals.

To us, one of the greatest *equippers* a leader can provide is education. And, leadership education should be at the top of all Splendid Leaders' lists. A highly visible demonstration of Equip People to Excel is to invest in leadership training and development of the workforce and the leader. It is the mark of a progressive, successful organization to maintain a healthy educational investment even in times of economic downturn. Often, during times of budget belt-tightening, corporate decision makers reduce or eliminate workforce education and training because it is viewed as a *nice to have* versus a necessary investment. But, it is precisely this investment that creates the opportunity for turnaround to more positive organizational performance in spite of depressed economics.

Below, we provide two examples of ways to Equip People to Excel: the leadership symposium and mentoring, coaching, and networking.

The Leadership Symposium

The influence of organizational leaders standing before their people and explaining what leadership qualities they expect from their workforce is incredibly powerful and a wonderful way to equip the workforce to excel. Evidence of this phenomenon is captured in an activity called the Leadership Symposium (LS) conducted at the Aeronautical Systems Center (ASC).

The LS was initiated when the senior leaders of ASC recognized in the early 2000s that their workforce of extremely well-educated, dedicated, and efficient program managers, engineers, financial specialists, contracting specialists, and support personnel needed to have better balance between their management and their leadership skills. The senior leaders believed the culture of the workforce was too heavily weighted in favor of efficient management.

> *As senior leaders in ASC at the time, we were concerned with how much emphasis the organization placed on management education and how little time was spent on leadership education.*

Thus, an effort was undertaken to create a workforce with better-balanced management and leadership training. In other words, the leadership embarked on a journey to invest in the leadership education of the workforce in order to change the organization's culture.

The approach for this leadership training involved several important, fundamental ideas:

1. Teaching effective leadership should include grounding in recognized, highly accepted, and well-documented research that has met the scrutiny of academia. ASC selected a popular leadership book to guide the organization and serve as the foundation for building a common understanding and language around leadership.

2. The teachers of the LS were selected organizational leaders. The use of these leaders to teach the workforce was significant for several important reasons:

   a. Leaders should be willing to invest their own time and energy to help *teach* leadership if they expect their employees to *study* leadship. It speaks volumes to the seriousness of the activity and to the commitment of the organization's leaders.

b. The senior leaders (teachers) worked and lived in the same environment as the employees (students), so they had firsthand experience and familiarity with the career paths to which the employee (student) aspired. Thus, the instructional stories the leaders (teachers) told were ones the employees (students) could readily relate to. Often the stories were about people the employees (students) actually knew, which made the leadership lessons come to life.

c. Leaders should have a vested interest in the well-being of the organization when they depart; therefore, training their replacements should be a priority.

d. When a significant number of leaders (teachers) and employees (students) participate in the LS, a common culture and *language of leadership* should emerge throughout the workforce.

It has been said that if you enlist the help of a segment of the workforce equal to at least the square root of N, where N is the total number of people in the workforce, the resultant number of people would be sufficient to change the culture of an entire organization. But, since one of us is an engineer, we say, in order to add a safety factor, it should be two times the square root of N! It is important to note, however, that the employees (students) involved in the initial cultural change activity should represent a diagonal cross section of the entire workforce.

3. Proven leaders were selected to teach a 2-3 hour session on the leadership lessons captured from the selected book. The leaders (teachers) were encouraged to be creative and to use whatever clasroom tools they felt appropriate to reinforce the lessons taught. But more importantly, they were told to tell stories from their work and private lives that illustrated the leadership concepts being taught.

The amount of senior leadership commitment to the LS was significant. It occasionally required some extra effort to recruit the leaders (teachers) because of their incredibly busy schedules. However, nearly every leader (teacher) would convey how much they enjoyed and learned from conducting their session--they were all eager to participate again. After all, Splendid Leaders want to serve; and what better way to serve than to share lessons learned!

The commitment exhibited by the senior leaders in assuming this leadership training touched the hearts of the workforce while simultaneously equipping people to excel. The responses from the employees (students) were overwhelmingly positive as measured by quantitative scoring and by individual feedback. The experience of the LS is a great example of the power that leaders' actions can have on creating, reinforcing, or changing workforce cultures and demonstrates what Splendid Leaders do.

Mentoring, Coaching, and Networking

Another equipper that enables people to excel is investing in relationship building through mentoring, coaching, and networking.

Mentoring is a personal relationship between a leader in the organization and an employee where a mutual exchange of learning occurs that contributes to both individuals' growth and development. The mentor is someone who is knowledgeable about the organization, is a recognized leader of the organization, and is *not* in the employee's chain of supervision. Both the mentor and the mentee must commit to the relationship and be willing to share beliefs and opinions honestly and openly. Mentoring is an opportunity for leaders to relate their career journeys--successes and pitfalls--in a spirit of learning for the mentee. The mentor serves as a sounding board and provides career guidance to the mentee. The richness of the mentoring relationship hinges on the communication skills of both parties. Mentoring programs range from highly formalized to very informal. The benefits of mentoring are many: (1) it attracts and retains employees; (2) it revitalizes leaders; (3) it provides a positive boost to the corporate culture; (4) it is an effective corporate communication tool; and (5) it contributes to a healthy workplace.

Coaching, much like mentoring, operates on the premise that every individual is a compilation of *gifts*. The purpose of coaching is to work with people to help them better understand the nature of their gifts and how to utilize them in their life. Relative to the workplace, coaching is employed to help people recognize their strengths and bring them to the forefront of daily work challenges. Supervisors and leaders use coaching techniques to enhance employees' performance. Coaches listen, probe, frame, evoke, teach, challenge, inspire, and strengthen those around them. Coaches do not *tell* employees what to do; coaches help employees *find* the solutions for themselves. Coaching enables employees to grow by transforming: (1) confusion to clarity; (2) fear to courage; (3) stagnation to growth; (4) mediocrity to passion; (5) reaction to proaction; and (6) passivity to accountability (Stroul 12-14).

Networking underscores the principle that no one is an island, and it is only by establishing a web of colleagues that one can reach his or her full potential. Networking can occur when planned events or gatherings allow for connecting with others to achieve a specific objective. Examples of networking opportunities include professional organizations, fundraisers, community activities, sporting events and social outings. Successful networking allows you to do your job better, understand organizational culture, politics, and changes as well as jump-start your career progression. Here are some do's and don'ts for effective networking.

<u>Do's</u>

Arrive Early

Have a Goal in Mind

Carry Business Cards/Resumes

Shake Hands and Make Eye Contact

Wear a Name Tag

Remember Names

Be Authentic

Bring a Positive Attitude

<u>Don'ts</u>

Be Reluctant to Approach People that You Don't Know

Solely Hang around Your Friends/Co-workers

Hard Sell Yourself

Give Up

Networking is directional. Learn to network *up* the organization with the leadership; *across* with peers inside and outside the organization; and *down* the organization with other employees. Networking relationships should be beneficial to all parties involved. Think about the purpose you desire to achieve and create payback to your networking partners.

Splendid Leaders recognize the value of mentoring, coaching, and networking as a means to Enable People to Excel. Splendid Leaders invest in opportunities to enhance their skill levels in mentoring, coaching, and networking to benefit their employees, their organization, and themselves. When leaders care about their employees' success and progression, the employees freely and reciprocally commit to doing all they can to make the organization successful. The return on investment of Enabling People to Excel is remarkable--try it!

Chapter 2.4

The Laws of Leadership

Use the Word Why

"Tell me and I forget;
show me and I remember;
ask why and I understand."
— unknown

Splendid Leaders love to ask why! They do this because they want to continuously improve the procedures and processes used to operate their organizations. A technique we often use when confronted with a procedure and process we want to improve is to ask, "Who developed the procedure or process?" If you can get to the person who authored the procedure or process, and if you can explain to that person why you think the procedure or process should be changed, you may find the author to be more receptive to the change than you expected. Remember, people who develop the procedures or processes are human beings who most often want to do the right thing. So give them a chance! If, however, that does not work, do not give up--go to the next level of appeal. One caution: you must be aware of the fine line between advocates of change, who use logic and reason to try to change things for the better, and zealots of change, who are fanatical in their approach and see no other solution but their own. Zealots often do not listen to reason. No one enjoys working with zealots.

Splendid Leaders often Use the Word *Why* in order to improve their organizations--and they support others in the organization who Use the Word *Why* to seek improvements.

BE CLEAR ON HOW YOU ASK WHY?

When Vince was leading a large research organization, he and other senior leaders spent several painful weeks each year formulating the annual budget. The process in place at the time required him and the leadership team to listen to briefing after briefing reflecting all the great ideas the workforce had for investing money to pursue technological advances.

There were always more valid ideas for using budget dollars than there were budget dollars. After nearly three weeks of listening, the leadership team took another week to deliberate and finalize the budget. Needless to say, Vince wanted to find a more efficient way to accomplish this task, and hopefully, free up the leadership team's time. So, he asked why the large time commitment and the painful process were needed. To answer this question, the organization established a team from a diagonal cross section of employees involved in the process; allowed them to select their own leader; gave them access to relevant data; and asked them to create a better process.

> *Some of you may recall this was the approach used during the Total Quality movement of the '80s and '90s.*

46

After several months, the team was ready to present the results of their work to Vince and the leadership team. The process team had selected a young engineer, Laura Rea, as their leader. Laura explained what her team had done and concluded with something like: "Dr. Russo, we have solved the budget process problem, and we are about to free up four weeks each year for you and the leadership team!" Needless to say, Vince and the leadership team were anxious to hear the solution. Laura went on to say that since the process improvement team had been asked to *fix* the process, they had decided they would relieve Vince and the leadership team of the responsibility to construct the budget each year, and she and the process improvement team would do it instead! Obviously, Laura and her team misinterpreted Vince's "why" question. They concentrated on changing *who* spent the long time and suffered the pain of the process and not on *how* to improve the existing budget process. Needless to say, the team was asked to continue their efforts by providing other options.

Splendid Leaders routinely Use the Word *Why* to improve operational procedures and processes as well as to teach employees the importance of opening their minds to new possibilities by the use of one, small word, *Why*.

Chapter 2.5

The Laws of Leadership

Have Fun!

"If you don't make the workplace fun,
You limit your ability to lead."
— Vincent J. Russo

We have observed many good leaders in our careers. We have read many books about effective leadership. We have taken many leadership classes from well-known academic institutions. We have asked many people about what characteristics they have observed in their favorite leaders. We have studied the research of well-known leadership experts. Based on these sources and our personal experiences, we are convinced that <u>Have Fun!</u> is one tenet that is neither talked nor written about nearly enough, let alone routinely actualized in workplace behavior. We firmly believe that Splendid Leaders create an environment where people enjoy coming to work each day--in other words, they have fun in the workplace. Now, by having fun, we do not mean you tell jokes all day nor have parties at the end of each work day. Rather, we mean the environment created by Splendid Leaders should be one where employees wake up each morning and say to themselves, "I look forward to going to work today." At the end of the day, they say, "I am glad I work here because I did something worthwhile today, and it was appreciated." We cannot emphasize enough the *was appreciated* part of the previous statement. Remember, work and fun are not the antithesis of one another.

Splendid Leaders create a workplace where incredible achievements occur routinely in an environment replete with fun. Fun comes in many flavors--it can be relaxed surroundings where people can tastefully tease or josh each other; where appropriate practical jokes are experienced; and where amusing activities are enjoyed. Fun in our personal and professional lives contributes to our physical and emotional health. There is plenty of research supporting the assertion that fun and laughter release good-feeling endorphins. On the emotional health side, fun and laughter also reduce the negative impact of work stressors. As Dale Carnegie said, "People rarely succeed unless they have fun in what they are doing."

As part of an Air Force Institute of Technology survey, employees were asked to describe an experience where a leader exhibited behavior that best represented the concept of Have Fun! in the workplace (Thurston). The results produced two key elements that constitute a fun environment:

(1) *Allow humor to reduce stress and boredom*. This refers to leadership behaviors that encourage humor to break tension and

create an enjoyable workplace. The employees who participated in this study were able to recognize the extent that a leader (a) allows humor to break through during tense moments, (b) encourages nonoffensive humor as a way to make the workplace more fun, (c) is not afraid to laugh at himself/herself, and (d) is willing to laugh and have fun with others.

(2) *Promote fun activities to relax and unwind*. This refers to leadership behaviors that encourage creative and fun activities to increase morale and job satisfaction. The employees were able to recognize the extent that leaders (a) encourage simple, quick and fun activities that lift spirits at work, (b) find ways to offset hardships caused by work with some fun outcome or activity, (c) take advantage of lulls in schedule for relaxing and fun activities, and (d) are willing to take a break during busy periods to do something fun as a unit.

Here are some ideas on how to have fun in the workplace.

Birthday Parties

A monthly party for all the members of your organization who have birthdays in the same month is an easy, inexpensive way to Have Fun! At these parties, do something that allows the group to enjoy each other's company in addition to serving light refreshments. For instance, go on the Web and learn something that happened on their birthdays in the year of their birth and review your findings with the group. Make it a game by seeing who can guess the correct answers to questions based on the events of that year; e.g., guess the top song, the most popular movie, other great people born on the same day, and the cost of a gallon of gas or a loaf of bread.

Popcorn Meetings

When in charge of a meeting you anticipate will be unusually difficult, put a large bowl of popcorn in the middle of the conference table. It is hard to explain why, but people just seem to be less testy with a large bowl of popcorn sitting in front of them. We believe this happens because people associate popcorn with fun or happy times: movies, ball games, campfires, and parties. There may also be some physiological reasons for this effect since popcorn is believed to contain chemicals known to cause more mellow behavior by releasing endorphins. So, the next time you approach a contentious issue, fire up the popcorn maker!

Childhood Pictures

Another fun-promoting technique, utilized by our good friend, Bob Raggio, was showing early childhood pictures of staff meeting attendees. He obtained early (the earlier the better) pictures of senior leaders from their families and asked the staff meeting attendees to try to identify the leaders pictured. No matter whose picture was shown, it inevitably brought about laughter, creative comments, and humorous comparisons between the current looks of the person at the staff meeting and their early childhood photo. Always share the pictures at the beginning of meetings to help set a *fun* tone for the rest of the session.

Celebrations

Celebrations are a traditional way to Have Fun! with your fellow workers. Going out to lunch or dinner to celebrate a successful year, the achievement of a challenging goal or a promotion is a fairly easy thing to do.

For more elaborate celebrations, we suggest ones where various units of the organization compete against each other using a theme. One illustrative example we experienced was a Mardi Gras parade float contest. Each unit created a float and judges awarded prizes based upon various categories such as most unique, most recognizable, and most ugly. The level of fun involved in preparation and teamwork that went into this celebration was amazing. And, long after the celebration had passed, everyone had even more fun debating who *really* should have won the prizes!

Be forewarned, photos of these celebrations have a way of resurfacing to prolong the fun!

Other effective examples to Have Fun! include: cook-offs; golf outings; indoor minature golf tournaments; Family Feud; Trivial Pursuit; picnics; sporting competitions; and ball-game outings.

A DIFFERENT SURPRISE PARTY

Another friend of ours, Len Zeller, is fond of telling a story about a former boss who helped set the tone for fun in his organization. Len was invited to

53

a Saturday afternoon party at his boss' house. He arrived in shorts and a T-shirt, only to be greeted by the boss and his wife who where dressed in formal wear. Len, who thought he had misunderstood the proper attire for the occasion, was obviously highly embarrassed, and he quickly turned to leave in order to go home to change into formal wear. But, the boss called him back and quickly escorted him to the backyard where everyone was dressed in shorts and a T-shirt for the barbeque. The result, as Len expresses it, was that the boss set a tone that it was "OK" to have fun in the organization. The boss clearly created an environment where people enjoyed coming to work.

THE NUTCRACKER

For a holiday party, the leaders of an organization decided to put on a reenactment of a scene from *The Nutcracker*. Eight male senior leaders dressed in ballet costumes, including tutus and tights representing flowers; other leaders dressed as a bumblebee and as the Sugar Plum Fairy complete with wings, crown, pink tutu, and tights. A formal ballet instructor was enlisted to train the dancers. The uncharacteristic workplace ensemble did a 15 minute fully choreo-graphed dance to music from *The Nutcracker*. The ground rule was neither smiles nor laughter from the dancers was permitted--it was to be a "serious" performance. As the dancers moved around the stage, a 5-foot aluminum foil nutcracker descended from the ceiling. When the Sugar Plum Fairy reached for the nutcracker, the other dancers collected large cardboard replicas of walnuts. The fairy's role was to crack the nuts! Clearly this was an unconventional inter-pretation of *The Nutcracker*! As the dance continued, the bumblebee flitted about spreading "seeds." Near the end of the dance, each dancer grabbed a whipped cream pie, and the show ended with the bumblebee (the senior leader for the entire organization) getting eight pies in the face! Needless to say, the audience erupted into laughter and applause--they went wild! The ensemble was recognized with a standing ovation, and all the performers took an orches-trated bow followed by flowers for the fairy.

So what is the point of sharing the Nutcracker example? First, one of the best ways to Have Fun! in the workplace is to make fun of yourself--self-deprecating humor. The top leaders certainly did that.

Second, the preparation time for the leaders helped bond them as a team. And third, years later, everyone at the party still talked about the performance. An important lesson from this story is that in order to Have Fun!, it sometimes necessitates leaders making themselves vulnerable. When the leaders of an organization use self-deprecating humor, it defines them as human in the most basic way and unifies them with their employees--a powerful leadership tool.

Chapter 2.6

The Laws of Leadership

Cast a Splendid Shadow

"Every organization is, in effect,
the lengthened shadow of its leader."
— *Thomas Lipton*

The sixth leadership tenet, Cast a Splendid Shadow, has to do with leaders living the values and norms that represent the desired culture of the organization. There is no doubt that actions of the leader speak loudly, and by his or her actions, a leader demonstrates on a daily basis his or her leadership beliefs--and these beliefs are frequently mirrored by the entire workforce.

No matter what a leader does, it will be reflected in the behavior and attitudes of all who work for him or her. Unfortunately, that means all of the leader's actions, irrespective of whether the actions are good or bad. So good or bad, a leader's actions will be observed and reflected by the behaviors of the workforce.

Another aspect of Cast a Splendid Shadow is recognizing that leadership is about serving others. Some people may not relate positively to the word serve as a leadership characteristic. They tend to associate serve with servitude. But remember, servitude has to do with accomplishing what others demand; whereas, service has to do with passionately providing what others need. Much like other professionals, such as artists, ministers, teachers, writers, missionaries, and physicians, serving others in any capacity is sometimes referred to as a *calling*. The role of a leader is a very high calling (Hunter 27). In other words, leaders have a significant impact on the lives of those they lead. The role of the leader is not to rule with an iron fist and dominate others; the role of the leader is to serve (Hunter 62). As previously noted, leadership is about getting things done through people. Thus, the relationship between leaders and employees is at the heart of serving. When leaders approach the relationship from a perspective of *serving* the organization and the people, they demonstrate the tenet of Cast a Splendid Shadow. Serving is not thinking less of yourself; it is thinking about yourself less (Hunter 111). As Albert Schweitzer said: "If you truly desire happiness, seek and learn how to serve."

A COACH'S SPLENDID SHADOW

For the first three seasons that Vince played football at the University of Rochester, his head coach was Elmer Burnham. Coach Burnham was from the old school of hard-nosed, intimidating coaching, and he was very successful, including an unbeaten season in 1958. Unfortunately, between Vince's junior and senior years, Coach Burnham retired, so the assistant coach, Paul Bitgood, assumed responsibility as head coach. The coaching styles of these two individuals were miles apart. Coach Bitgood was a gentleman's gentleman. He treated all the players with respect, care, and warmth. He was viewed as a father figure, and everyone wanted the 1961 team to be as good as the ones led by Coach Burnham.

The first game of Coach Bitgood's head coaching career was a tough one--and a loss. Vince and his co-captain, Tony Stranges, took the loss personally, and in the locker room after the game, they both sat in the corner teary-eyed. The two young football players felt they had disappointed Coach Bitgood. Here is how Vince remembers Coach Bitgood's reaction, "When he approached the two of us, I thought we may be in for a tongue lashing. Instead, he praised our efforts; he said he was proud of us; he reassured us that it was only a game; and he said he believed in the team and in us. I wish I could remember his exact words because they were, in my mind, truly representative of how best to lead. However, I can remember our response--we were inspired to keep working hard and to believe good things would happen. Our football team had a successful winning season; but more importantly, the life-long lesson of the power of compassion and love are still with me today. I often remember Coach Bitgood's behavior when I find myself feeling disappointed. It serves to reenergize and encourage me as a leader as well as a person."

At the introduction to this chapter, we referenced a quote by Thomas Lipton regarding the importance of casting a shadow. In other words, organizations reflect the *good* and the *bad* elements of the shadow cast by the leader. Because we can also learn by observing negative actions, here is a story about *what not to do*!

A NEGATIVE SHADOW

One of the most demoralizing negative actions we have seen taken by a leader concerned an attempt to launch a new organizational development concept. This action involved assembling approximately 150 key leaders of a large organization to listen to invited experts present a new idea that the leader wanted to implement. Prior to the meeting, the leader built expectations that this would be a watershed event for the organization. When all were assembled, the leader heightened expectations by saying how important this new concept would be to the future of the organization, and how he wanted everyone to pay close attention to what the experts had to say. Then, as he ended his opening remarks, he announced he had another commitment and would not return for the rest of the day! You could just feel the huge letdown by the assembled key members. He wanted his subordinates to pay attention, but he had other more pressing tasks at that time--a good example of how not to Cast a Splendid Shadow.

The sixth leadership tenet, Cast a Splendid Shadow, is rooted in past history as evident in the following anecdote about Saint Francis of Assisi (1181-1226): The early followers of Saint Francis wanted to know what to do when they went out into the streets. Saint Francis told them, "Preach the Gospel at all times. If necessary, use words."

Splendid Leaders communicate by example. They demonstrate the behaviors they want others to emulate--they Cast a Splendid Shadow.

Chapter 3.1

Harnessing the Strength of Emotions

The Soft Stuff Is the Hard Stuff

"Getting what you want,
rather than taking what you get."
— Kaye and Jordan Evans

Up to this point, our discussions have centered on the "hard" side of Splendid Leadership. The hard side involves all those concepts, skills, and abilities that are externally focused and demonstrated by an individual within an organizational construct. Now, we are going to explore the "soft" side of the Splendid Leader with an inward focus on the leader, as well as the workforce being led.

Splendid Leaders move organizations in the right direction, ignite passion to achieve organizational success, and inspire people to do their best. We have examined the first two pillars of Splendid Leadership, Behavior Realities and Leadership Tenets. Now, we will look at the third pillar, **Essence of Leaders**. Even before explaining this concept, we realize that the reading audience will fall into one of the following three camps. Some of you already understand and practice the Essence of Leaders in your personal and professional lives. Some of you have closed your minds and hearts to the Essence of Leaders and are busy developing ways to discount what will follow. You may be thinking, "It's just more of that 'touchy feely' stuff."

> *Too bad--you're cheating yourselves and those you interact with from some truly enlightening experiences.*

And finally, some of you will awaken a desire to understand the Essence of Leaders and to master it!

> *Way to go--a life-altering leadership experience may await you.*

Let's begin with a definitional approach to *essence*. According to Daniel Webster, *essence* is the "spirit, core, heart, and soul of something." On a more humorous side, Emeril Lagasse, world-renowned chef, refers to *essence* as the secret ingredient in a recipe that "steps it up" a notch or two with a resounding "BAM!" And, according to Splendid Leaders, *essence* is "the leadership advantage or edge that separates the ordinary from the extraordinary." Therefore, essence enables Splendid Leaders to create personal and organizational success.

We define *essence* as "the ability to make feelings work to achieve desired results by using emotions to facilitate exceptional performance from oneself and from others." The academic underpinning of essence can be found in the works of Daniel Goleman and others in their studies of emotional intelligence. It has been proven to be as important, if not more important, in job and leadership success than intellect (Boyatzis, Goleman, McKee 27-28).

> *Now, we know that some people begin to squirm when talking about feelings. So, we're going to spend some time helping you get more comfortable!*

Unfortunately, society applies pressure in personal and professional environments to suppress feelings or emotions--especially for men. Typically, when we ask employees to identify feelings that are present in their work environments, employees respond with some fairly elementary emotions: happy, glad, sad, mad, or angry. They run out of examples very quickly. They just normally do not think about feelings and work simultaneously. To most people, work is a place that concentrates on producing products and services, not a place for emotions to reside, be identified, recognized, and utilized. We hope this pillar will help you realize the limitation this creates in one's ability to lead. Emotions can be very powerful in improving performance to achieve goals in the workplace and in your personal life.

Let's tune our senses into workplace emotions. They are present whether acknowledged or not, so let's bring them out into the open. Here is an example of an emotional inventory present in the typical workplace.

Abandoned	Combative	Foolish	Humble
Afraid	Confident	Frantic	Ignored
Adrift	Cynical	Friendly	Impatient
Aggravated	Defensive	Furious	Impulsive
Ashamed	Defiant	Gentle	Inadequate
Bashful	Despondent	Gloomy	Intense
Belittled	Devoted	Gullible	Jealous
Carefree	Eager	Happy	Joyful
Cavalier	Empty	Hateful	Kind
Coerced	Envious	Helpless	Lazy
Lethargic	Nervous	Quiet	Selfish
Listless	Neglected	Reactive	Timid
Lost	Numb	Rejected	Thrilled
Lucky	Open	Relaxed	Trapped
Mad	Ornery	Resentful	Uneasy
Merry	Paranoid	Resolute	Valued
Miffed	Patient	Rotten	Wary
Miserable	Peeved	Sassy	Withdrawn
Moody	Playful	Secure	Welcome
Naïve	Powerful	Shamed	Zapped

Figure 3.1.0

This is only a partial list! Is it any wonder that leadership is a complex art, considering employees come to work each day bringing with them a plethora of emotions? Social scientists have documented many more distinct emotions in the workplace. These emotions do not necessarily originate in the workplace, but they certainly could. The point is they coexist with efforts to deliver products and services. The worst approach a leader could use is to ignore this emotional repertoire in the workplace. Splendid Leaders spend time understanding, recognizing, and relating feelings to productive behaviors in the workplace. They use emotions to make the organization's products and services even better. We believe Splendid Leadership occurs when the head (thought) and the heart (feelings) meet (Boyatzis, Goleman, McKee 26).

The Essence of Leaders, in reality, is science based--which brings us to a condensed lesson in physiology to help us truly understand the concept. Without getting too technical, the human brain is made up of two neural systems: one for intellect and one for emotion. The systems are separate but related (Boyatzis, Goleman, McKee 27). Intellect resides in the neocortex. This is the center for technical knowledge, business acumen, logic, and concepts, as well as analytical skills. Emotion resides in the limbic system of the brain (Goleman 97). It governs instinct, feelings, gut reactions, and the all too familiar reactions of fight, flee or freeze. Feelings lubricate the intellect. In fact, the neocortex evolved from the limbic system. Studies have shown that one person's feelings emit signals that can affect another person's hormones, sleep patterns, cardiovascular system, and immune system (Boyatzis, Goleman, McKee 46). Now, that is a commanding signal!

> *We were researching the concept of essence and found this description, by neuropsychiarist, Louann Brizendine, of neuron operations as it applies to gender brain differences: "Women have an eight-lane superhighway for processing emotions, while men have a small country road" (Brizendine). The neurons are traversing between the neocortex and the limbic systems for both genders, just at different rates!*

Often, emotions can be more powerful than intellect. Neurons operate back and forth traversing the brain's neurological highway. Thus, intellect and emotion are intrinsically interconnected. Splendid Leaders recognize this and are skilled in using both neural systems of the brain for unsurpassed organizational and personal results. By now, you may have realized that our reference to the soft side of leadership, the Essence of Leaders, is science based; i.e., the soft stuff is really the hard stuff!

Chapter 3.2

Harnessing the Strength of Emotions

The Five Elements of Essence

"What lies behind us and what lies before us are tiny matters,
compared to what lies within us."
— Oliver Wendell Holmes

Splendid Leaders can be created. All it takes is knowledge, understanding, and practice to reform preconceived notions or outdated behavior habits into the essence of Splendid Leadership. The elements of essence are shown in Figure 3.2.0 (Goleman 95).

Figure 3.2.0

When reviewing the five elements of the Essence of Leaders, one quickly recognizes that the first three elements have to do with "self," while the last two elements relate to "others." Thus, in order to possess the Essence of Leaders, you must devote time and effort into understanding yourself in order to enable you to understand others. Self-awareness, as the word connotes, has to do with knowing your emotional self first. Self-management is the next step following the attainment of Self-awareness. It deals with managing one's emotions to demonstrate personal behavior that contributes to achieving organizational and personal goals. Self-motivation takes Self-management one step further by using one's emotions to elicit desired actions. To illustrate, Peter Luongo, former CEO of the Berry Company and nationally acclaimed speaker, says, "There is no such thing as motivating others. Motivation is very personal and derived from within an individual. Each of us has the responsibility to motivate ourselves. Leaders not only motive themselves, but also inspire others." To elaborate further, think of motivation as intrinsically derived, and inspiration as the result of the extrinsic actions of leaders.

The next two elements of the Essence of Leaders turn from an inward or personal focus to an outward focus on others. Interpersonal Expertise has to do with understanding the emotions of others, as well as how their emotions drive their behavior. Thus, this element of essence ties directly to the first pillar of Splendid Leadership, Behavior Realities, by providing a basis for understanding the underlying emotions that cause people to behave the way they do. The final element of the

Essence of Leaders is Relationship Building. This entails taking the knowledge of what drives the behavior of others in the workplace and employing that knowledge to create and reinforce alliances with the leaders, employees, and teams within an organization. In the simplest of terms, personal and professional life is a series of relationships, and the health of these relationships directly relates to one's success.

The following is a more in-depth look at each of the elements of the Essence of Leaders.

Self-Awareness

According to Daniel Goleman, a leading authority in the field of emotional intelligence, Self-awareness is the ability to read and understand your emotions as well as recognize their impact on work performance and relationships (Boyatzis, Goleman, McKee 30). Self-awareness is the foundation of all the other elements of essence. Through introspection, Self-awareness allows us to discover our emotional strengths and limitations. Self-awareness tends to be a skill that is developed later in life--if at all. Therefore, to practice Self-awareness earlier in life takes time, dedication, and determination, possibly without a clear understanding of the worth of the investment. This investment will be worth the effort to you and those who are important to you. Here's why: acquiring the ability to recognize and be attuned to your emotions, allows you to alter those emotions from negative to positive. These positive emotions can then drive desired, productive behaviors by you. Once you become practiced in modifying your emotions to drive your behaviors, the understanding can then be applied to affecting the behaviors of others.

Most organizations believe that to change employee behavior, all you have to do is have the CEO articulate the desired behavior; make it part of the performance reward system; and expect all the employees of the organization to demonstrate the articulated behavior. Unfortunately, this approach does not work because emotions, not mandates, drive behavior.

> *Recall in Chapter 1.1, we emphasized that emotions, evoked by Anticipatory Realities are powerful influencers of behavior.*

If a leader, or anyone else in the workplace, comes to work wrought with "defensive" feelings (pick a negative emotion--any one from the list), they will be consumed with responding to this emotion. They will not trust the people around them. They will be "watching their backs." They will look for the pitfalls instead of the opportunities that come before them. They will be dysfunctional in teams. They will be consumed with a negative attitude. How do you think this will affect the delivery of products and services generated or the interface with the consumers of these products and services?

Self-awareness begins with self-reflection. This is a rather personal activity, and therefore, varies by individual. Some people do their best self-reflection while taking a walk in the woods, performing yoga, journaling, biking, or doing whatever calms their mind and spirit so they can learn more about themselves. These activities are called the *triggers* to Self-awareness. Find your trigger, exercise it, and begin your journey. The journey to richer Self-awareness begins by tuning into that *voice* in your head. The internal conversation generated by that voice deals with questions and answers about your personal values, beliefs, qualities, characteristics, norms, and opinions. This conversation is followed by that timeless question: Why? And, then, the conversation with oneself starts all over again! So goes the path to Self-awareness. Don't be surprised if during these conversations you find yourself revisiting and replowing the same ground seeking truth and understanding. Delving into your Self-awareness does not come easily and requires practice. Some people find it helpful to capture the sense of these nonverbal conversations in written or electronic format. This allows you to refer to and take stock of your emotions in order to sensitize yourself to the feelings that you carry around and the event that activates these feelings. Once you name the emotion(s), you have the opportunity to nourish or change the emotion(s). Then, you can learn to control (manage) your emotion(s).

Self-Management

Self-management is another way of saying emotional self-control. Managing your emotions allows you to be adaptable to changing situations in order to overcome obstacles. Self-management involves keeping disruptive emotions and impulses under control while leveraging positive emotions (Boyatzis, Goleman, McKee 39). It also entails the unique capacity to soothe oneself. This is the ability to shake off gloom, anxiety, anger, irritation, and other negative feelings. Why spend time with non-productive feelings--especially when the capacity to alter such feelings lies within your grasp? A collection of feelings shapes your mood, and your mood shows up before you do!

There are many techniques for controlling and redirecting moods, such as sleeping on it, consciously forcing yourself to stay calm in rough waters, postponing actions until your mood changes, or demonstrating the courage to change decisions made while experiencing negative moods. One effective mechanism is to find *your place to go*. This is often called the mental vacation. Close your eyes, relax, take a few deep breaths, and envision a place that brings you a sense of calm and control. By way of an example, nothing beats the soothing effect of clear blue, warm ocean water with the waves lapping at a white sandy shore. Visualize the azure-blue ocean; taste the sea salt on your lips; feel the warmth of the sun on the beach by running your toes through the sand; hear the roar of the waves rushing upon the shore. You may have to pinch yourself to return to reality. A few minutes in *your place*, and you are ready to manage your emotions effectively and tackle any issue.

Self-Motivation

Taking Self-management one step further lands us in the arena of Self-motivation (Boyatzis, Goleman, McKee 39). By way of reconnecting to the lessons of Behavior Realities as captured in Chapter 1, use of Anticipatory Realities is an effective tool for motivating yourself and inspiring others. Self-motivation is a form of "self-talk." It involves labeling the emotions you are experiencing and leveraging these emotions to achieve the desired personal behaviors that enable you to attain your goals. Encouraging yourself to be optimistic in the face of setbacks or seeing the positives in distressing situations are examples of Self-motivation. Practicing Self-motivation entails harnessing one's feelings to accomplish desired end objectives.

NOT THAT JOB!

Have you ever been at the point in your career where you have the dream job? Where you have carefully surrounded yourself with competent, driven performers; where the processes are lean and responsive; where the work is creative, fulfilling, and challenging; where the customer is singing your praises; where life could not get any better? Well, that is where Donna was midway into her career. She loved coming to work each day and so did the rest of the team. She wanted to stay in that environment for the rest of her career.

And then, the dreaded phone call was received from her boss. Her boss informed her that corporate leadership had deemed it time for her to move on to a bigger, better assignment. She was thinking, "It does not get any better than this job." He went on to relay that she would be moving to the number one job in her career field. He did not have to say anymore. It was a well-known fact among her peers that this job was a killer--unbelievable overtime, high stress, constant travel, lots of second guessing by higher ups, uncooperative suppliers, unreasonable customers, undersized staff because no one wanted to work in that environment, and oh yes, the organizational leader was a fire-breathing dragon with an abusive, intimidating style of leadership!

She immediately responded that she was flattered; however, she still had many goals to achieve before considering her current job to be complete. She suggested offering the vacant job to one of her peers who had not changed jobs as frequently as she had. Her boss confirmed that he had already tried these points with upper management to no avail. Put bluntly, Donna was directed to move to the new job within two weeks. During those two weeks, she had plenty of time to process the emotions that she was feeling: fear, anger, denial, abandonment, regret, dismay, frustration, betrayal, and irritation. Not exactly the frame of mind that is conducive to tackling a new assignment with vigor and enthusiasm! Since she recognized that feelings not only drive behaviors, but also are highly contagious and often reflected back, she had some serious self-motivation work to do before greeting her new supervisor and new team. Donna took the time to just think about how she wanted to "show up." Her priorities were clear: (1) ensure the mission was accomplished in an outstanding manner; (2) shield the team from any abusive behaviors; (3) create a healthy and appreciative environment to perform the work; and (4) try to survive! She thought about the emotions that she wanted to display in this new position: enthusiasm, confidence, commitment, optimism, creativity, support, and lightheartedness. Donna tried to re-create the feelings one experiences on their best day at work as a proxy for how she would approach this new job. She promised herself to take frequent readings on her emotions to keep the positive feelings in place. In other words, Donna used the concept of self-motivation to get through this assignment. She credits self-motivation for driving the necessary behaviors and resultant actions that enabled her to be successful in the new job.

Interpersonal Expertise

The last two elements of the Essence of Leaders move the focus from oneself to others. Interpersonal Expertise refers to the ability to understand the emotions or feelings of others in order to relate in a positive, effective way to achieve desired results. Interpersonal Expertise consists of sensing the emotions of others in order to understand their perspectives and truly relate to their concerns. In order to be successful at interpersonal expertise, a leader must possess a high degree of empathy as well as the ability to establish caring connections. It is important for leaders to be able to spot emotions in others because, like attitude, emotions are highly contagious in both a positive or negative manner. Thus, leaders want to leverage the benefits of positive feelings in the workforce and be instrumental in changing negative feelings into more constructive emotions.

Emotions are like mirrors. People reflect and escalate the emotions directed at them, which underscores once again the importance and impact of Self-awareness. In dealing with emotions, a leader must employ artful communication skills such as active listening, negotiating, persuading, resolving conflict and building consensus. By way of illustration, what if someone is demonstrating cynicism in the workplace by commenting, "This stinks. This is really a terrible, shoddy, amateurish product/process/idea. This will never work. I'm appalled at being associated with a team that produces such an inferior product/process/idea." One positive response could be a calmly delivered question, "What part do you dislike the most, and let's work on that first?" This diffuses the emotion and reorients the cynic to solution-based teamwork. It also reduces conflict by recognizing the emotion and indicating a desire to make a midcourse correction. At other times, when the leader senses the overpowering presence of negative, destructive emotions in one or more individuals, the best course of action may be to call for a time-out. This allows for a cooling-off period when clearer heads may make a more concerted effort to discuss the issue.

Leaders with strong interpersonal expertise recognize that everyone has a set of filters from their life experiences that are used to process verbal and nonverbal communication. These filters are unique to every individual because they are based upon the same elements that drive behavior, as noted in Chapter 1, Historical Realities. Splendid Leaders focus on understanding their own filters, as well as the filters of those with whom they interact, as a way to strengthen their Interpersonal Expertise.

Relationship Building

Once the employee knows you want to enable them to excel, then you are ready to build a relationship. A robust and richly productive personal and professional life depends on strong relationships. Relationships are structured around desired intent and outcome. They thrive when the parties in the relationship establish a strong rapport and nourish the relationship by deliberately building bonds. Leaders, adept at Relationship Building, typically possess expertise in the areas of collaboration, teamwork, listening, conflict resolution, and communication. They also recognize that practicing self-disclosure introduces a vulnerability that solidifies trust in relationships. Self-disclosure by a leader has a way of breeding self-disclosure among the participants of the relationship, knitting them together. When a leader reveals his or her vulnerabilities, the leader becomes more humanistic, more approachable and connects with employees or teams in a meaningful way. Here are some examples of leaders' self-disclosures:

I don't have all the answers. I need to hear from you.

I am not sure where to start. Any suggestions?

I really start to sweat when I have to give a presentation. I appreciate your understanding.

I need help with strategic thinking. Please pitch in.

I dislike giving negative feedback. You'll have to bear with me. I tend to over think decisions. Prompt me to stay on point.

Do you not just *feel* the barriers between individuals diminishing? Are you encouraged to share your carefully concealed vulnerabilities?

There are a whole host of skills associated with strong Relationship Building. For example, supportive listening is the bedrock of Relationship Building. This aptitude enables parties in the relationship to listen for clarification, reflection, and understanding. Another valued proficiency in building relationships is the ability to diffuse tense situations to de-escalate disagreements. This involves creating calm through identifying negative emotions and applying conflict resolution techniques. For example, if one party of a relationship is momentarily out-of-control, offer some diversionary comments such as: Let's sit down and pause for a moment. Could you speak a little slower--I want to make sure I hear all your points. Or, I want to carefully consider all your thoughts--could you go over them again for me?

One of the most important ingredients in a robust relationship is time, a scarce commodity in today's world. Making time for those in a relationship, whether at home or at work, is a gift that pays enduring benefits.

If leaders want to realize different employee behaviors for better team interaction, improved customer relations, enhanced creativity or sustained strategic growth, then they must become more adept at reading and influencing the emotions of those in the workplace in order to affect their behavior.

MOVE HIM OR FIX HIM

The Vice President of Operations (Bob) of a large organization had enormous responsibilities and a handpicked team to help him execute the organization's mission. One valued team member was the Director of Sales (Tim) who was responsible for a 100 person sales force covering a six-region district that was directly responsible for over $800 million in revenues. The performance of the sales force was instrumental to the success of the company's mission.

One day, the Vice President for Marketing (Max) was visited by Bob who had a specific request. Bob wasted no time getting right to the point. He expressed his dissatisfaction with Tim's recent performance. According to Bob, "It's a complete mystery to me. How can someone be so energetic and outstanding one minute and a supportive, contributing team member; then totally shut down and ignore his responsibilities?" Max was stunned, and asked Bob whether he had discussed his observations with Tim. Bob said the time for talk was over, and he wanted Tim either "moved or fixed." This was a very sensitive situation because Max and Tim not only had a close professional relationship, but also were long-time personal friends. In fact, Max had recommended Tim for the Director of Sales position several years earlier. Bob abruptly left Max's office for more pressing matters.

Max immediately invited Tim to his office for a follow-up session. Max decided to get Tim's perspective by initiating the conversation with, "How are things going for you?" Tim seemed preoccupied with other thoughts, but responded that things were okay--the usual. Max relayed that Bob had paid him a visit to discuss Tim's performance. Opening the floodgates, Tim seemed annoyed and had nothing positive to relate regarding Bob's leadership and more specifically, their relationship. Tim felt Bob did not care about his people and could not be trusted. He went on to say that he no longer respected Bob and that Bob was only interested in meeting sales quotas.

Max was surprised to witness such an emotional outburst from Tim. Max asked Tim whether he could pinpoint when the relationship had begun to unravel. Tim paused as if trying to muster up the courage to continue. Finally, Tim revealed that his mother, who had single-handedly raised a family of three after his father passed away, recently lost her battle with cancer. It was obvious that Tim had a special reverence and admiration for his mother. He went on to say that Bob never acknowledged his loss and did not attend the viewing, the funeral, or express his condolences with a card or e-mail. In Tim's words, "How can anyone work for a boss like that?"

Max shared this information with Bob. Bob was dumbfounded. According to Bob, the office had sent several expressions of condolences including flowers, taking dinner over for the family, and house-sitting during the viewing and funeral. Max explained that Tim needed a personal expression from him. Bob pointed out he had piled the work on Tim so that he could bury himself with work in order to overcome his grief. Bob felt work was soothing and would substitute a sense of accomplish for the emptiness that accompanies such a loss. Max sensed Bob had really thought about Tim's situation in a very caring way. Max and Bob talked about how different people grieve in different ways. Bob acknowledged that he would like to retract his original request to "move him or fix him," because he wanted to take a shot at mending a relationship that he valued. Bob was not used to thinking and talking about emotions in the workplace. Bob asked for an opportunity to rebuild his relationship with Tim in order to keep a very talented Director of Sales in his organization. Even though Bob gave his best effort at repairing a damaged relationship, unfortunately, Tim requested reassignment. Sometimes, it is hard to undo unintentional damage to relationships that result from misunderstandings associated with strong emotions in the workplace. The broken relationship had nothing to do with Tim's output, but it had everything to do with his emotions at a critical time in his life.

Chapter 3.3

Harnessing the Strength of Emotions

Why Essence Counts

"Not everything that can be counted counts,
and, not everything that counts can be counted."
— Albert Einstein

Now that you have a working understanding of the five elements of the Essence of Leaders, it is appropriate to turn to the business world to gain a perspective of leaders who demonstrate essence. Lyle M. Spencer, president of Spencer Research, conducted a study of 300 CEOs who were asked to: (1) provide measures of corporate performance; (2) submit to a battery of emotional intelligence tests; and (3) participate in individual interviews (Cherniss, Goleman 1-2). The results enabled the study to identify the elite few CEOs who scored high in essence (emotional intelligence) and were deemed the "superstars." Examination of the superstars' companies indicated that their sales forces were 85 percent more productive; account managers generated 127 percent higher sales; and manufacturing supervisors trained in emotional intelligence managed a 17 percent more productive workforce. In other words, an understanding of the Essence of Leaders is a powerful attribute in the workplace. The understanding and practical application of essence has been credited for boosting innovation, enhancing the quality of decisions, making work more meaningful, improving business results, beating the competition, increasing the effectiveness of teams and transforming how people work together. Finally, essence enables leaders to attract and retain high-potential employees.

Understanding essence is highly useful in revealing the underlying emotions that define leadership styles. What is a leadership style? Leadership style is the persistent conduct or behavior that a leader demonstrates in the workplace. Behavioral scientists further elaborate by referring to leadership style as the habitual behavior reverted to during stressful situations.

To illustrate essence, let us dissect a few leadership styles (Goleman 82-90). Have you ever worked for the autocratic (do as I say) leader who has to be involved in even the minutest detail of the organization? This style is typified by a CEO who measured the distance between pictures hung in the lobby of the corporate headquarters building.

No kidding--this is a true recollection!

The autocratic leader possesses an emotional stockpile of fear, distrust, worry, apprehension, panic, alarm, concern, doubt, cynicism, and suspicion, feeding a sense of perfection and a desire for total control.

The democratic (tell me what you think) leader solicits the input of others in seeking the optimal path for the organization. The democratic leader enjoys emotions categorized by trust, openness, confidence, belief, sharing, frankness, sincerity, and faith in involving others to build consensus and promote cohesiveness in the workplace.

Finally, there is the collaborative (come with me) leader who mobilizes individuals and teams to achieve a shared organizational vision. The collaborative leader demonstrates empathy, harmony, caring, helpfulness, compassion, and sensitivity in moving people in the right direction.

This is by no means an exhaustive list of leadership styles. The point in identifying the emotions underlying the behavior of leaders is to emphasize the importance of essence in leadership. Perhaps Jack Strewmaker, retired president of Wal-Mart, captured the Essence of Leaders best when he said, "I don't care how much you know until you show me how much you care."

Chapter 4.1

Having It All; Not Doing It All!

Get Real!

"Some men see things as they are and say, 'Why?'
I dream of things that never were and say, 'Why not?'"
— *George Bernard Shaw*

The last pillar, **Life Balance**, rounds out the Splendid Leader. Until recently, the topic of life balance was not widely discussed in the workplace. People privately talked about components of life balance around the water cooler or at lunch, but seldom publicly in the workplace. Over the past 25 years, there has been an intensification of work driven by information technology, vulnerability to global competition, and the erosion of trust and loyalty within organizations that expect more from fewer workers with less value returned to the worker. These organizations mandated that, when at work, employees' attention and loyalty belong to the corporation. The subtle message was "make work your top priority and workplace success will be yours." Work and personal lives were traditionally seen as competing demands on leaders', managers', and employees' time (Graves, Ohlott, and Ruderman). That was the workplace of old; but we hope times are changing.

> *The source of some of the Life Balance pillar is based on the unpublished, joint research by Back and Haley as noted in Works Cited.*

What makes Life Balance an intriguing topic is that it applies to everyone irrespective of gender, race, ethnic origin, religion, economic situation, political persuasion, age, profession, or global location. A recent survey of 50,000 workers in the manufacturing and service industries showed 40 percent were dissatisfied with the balance between their work and their personal life (Hansen, 1). Marlene Buntings' book, *Willing Slaves*, noted that between 1977 and 1997, the average work-week increased 3.5 hours to 47.1 hours. In 2000, the Wheatley Study documented: 65 percent of workers said work was damaging their health; 77 percent said work was negatively affecting their relationship with their children; most couples spend more time at work than with each other; and the average person allocates 15 minutes per day on his or her social life (Buntings, 1-34). These statistics are signs that balancing work and life commitments is a growing problem. Splendid Leaders appreciate the implication of Life Balance and use it as a means to help their organizations thrive and prosper.

To personalize this pillar for your particular set of circumstances, let's have a little fun by answering the following questions:

> Do people tell you that you're a workaholic? Do you think that's a compliment?
>
> Do you take vacations without electronic devices?
>
> Do you skip lunch?
>
> What do you do for fun?
>
> What was the best day of your life?
>
> Do you struggle with recurring headaches/ stomachaches/backaches?
>
> Are you exhausted in the evenings?
>
> How would your family and friends describe you?
>
> Do you have feelings of guilt?
>
> Are you often sick on holidays?
>
> Do you go out to dinner in your work attire?
>
> Do you resent your colleagues who leave work on time?

If these questions resonate with you or if you cannot readily supply answers to these questions, then this pillar is for you! Research indicates that you are not alone as millions of individuals struggle with Life Balance daily. The good news is that through knowledge, understanding, and a willingness to change, you can alter your present situation and bring *balance* into your life.

Chapter 4.2

Having It All; Not Doing It All!

What Is Life Balance?

"Don't let making a living,
prevent you from making a life."
— John Wooden

Until recently, the literature and research in the area of Life Balance was extremely limited. In fact, most of the data originated "across the pond." Europe has been tuned into life balance as it relates to the workplace for some time. Thankfully, it is beginning to migrate to the United States and beyond as corporations and individuals begin to address this important concept. By definition, Life Balance is a *personal* blend of life commitments to optimize your full potential. In other words, working to live, not living to work. When you live to work, as some organizational cultures demand, you can miss out on life!

Some people assume that life balance is nothing more than time management. There are 24 hours in a day, 7 days in a week, which equals 168 hours per week allotted for Life Balance. From those 168 hours per week, let us subtract the typical: 50 hours for work, 49 hours for sleep, 20 hours to eat, 7 hours for personal hygiene, and 7 hours for commuting, which leaves 35 hours per week or 5 hours per day for *discretionary* use.

We recognize that your individual allocations may vary, so create your own discretionary total.

Anyway you cut it, that is not much time for all the demands that present themselves throughout a typical week. Life Balance is so much more than time management; it is what you *derive* from the things you do with the time you have (Galinsky 1).

Life Accounts

When discussing Life Balance, let us assume that each of us has four "life accounts": mental, physical, emotional, and spiritual. One could definitely identify many other life accounts (Zimmerman 38). However, for purposes of simplicity in explanation, we have chosen to categorize everything into four equally important accounts.

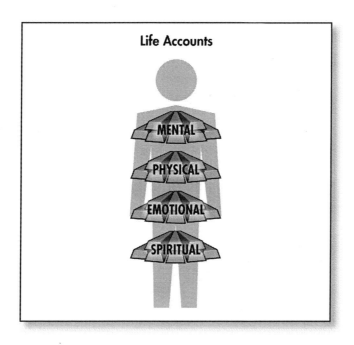

Figure 4.2.0

The mental account encompasses activities that stimulate the intellect and the ability to reason. For instance, educational pursuits, reading a book from the top ten nonfiction list, attending a technical seminar, or surfing the Web for information are all examples of investments in the mental life account.

The physical account has to do with interests that impact health and the body. The physical account is responsible for the well-being of your physiological make-up--your digestion, respiration, circulation, muscular, skeletal, nervous, vascular, endocrine, cardiac and intestinal systems. Attention to nutrition, exercise, regular physical check-ups, and taking yoga or health-conscious cooking classes all enhance the physical life account.

The emotional account links directly to the limbic system of the brain where feelings reside. Events that affect the emotional account include a promotion, marriage, the birth of a child or grandchild, death, divorce, an award, or retirement. The emotional account is key to healthy professional and personal relationships. It reflects how we feel about others and ourselves.

The spiritual account involves getting in touch with who you are throughout life's journey. It includes a multitude of topics, such as values, authenticity, faith and religious beliefs, as well as your purpose in life. The spiritual account is perhaps the most thought-provoking and often overlooked or neglected area. It requires self-reflection to reveal who you are and what you intend to do with your life.

Competing Commitments

Now that you understand what constitutes the life accounts, let's address the concept of competing commitments. We live in a highly complex personal and professional world where we are constantly bombarded by competing commitments. These competing commitments come from a multitude of sources; job, community, relationships, health, friends, and oneself. Here are some examples of competing commitments generated by each source.

Family: taxi children to activities, accompany an elderly parent to doctor, plan an anniversary celebration

Job: prepare a critical presentation, interview for a promotion, attend a two-week business trip

Community: collect for the fund drive, serve on the centennial committee, run for a Board of Education

Relationships: undergo a divorce, attend a church meeting, support a neighborhood project

Health: run in a half-marathon, keep a dental appointment, prepare healthy meals, have a colonoscopy

Friends: go to a sports event, go bike riding, go out to dinner

Oneself: read a good book, go to a movie, exercise, attend a cooking class, go fishing, meditate, play golf

Clearly, this is by no means a complete list, but you get the idea. The obvious conclusion is that with just five discretionary hours in a day, all of your competing commitments will not be met to your expectations.

Each of these commitments can be viewed as having a positive or negative effect on the four life accounts. They either make "deposits" into or "withdrawals" from the life accounts. It is quite possible for a single commitment to have both a positive and a negative effect on different life accounts. For example, assume that you are earning a master's degree by taking night classes. That commitment would definitely register a deposit into your mental account--you are growing and developing in your intellectual capacity. However, in order to study, prepare research papers, attend group work, and meet the other demands of a master's program, you may be spending less time with your family, which registers a withdrawal from your emotional account. Additionally, you may be getting less sleep, adding an attendant negative impact on your physical account. It's important to take the time to identify these competing commitments, to recognize them correctly as deposits or withdrawals and to work toward equilibrium over time.

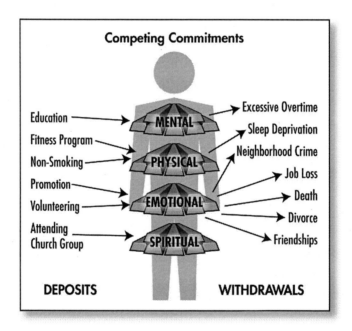

Figure 4.2.1

The Process

Let's tie together the concepts that have been introduced so far with the following illustration:

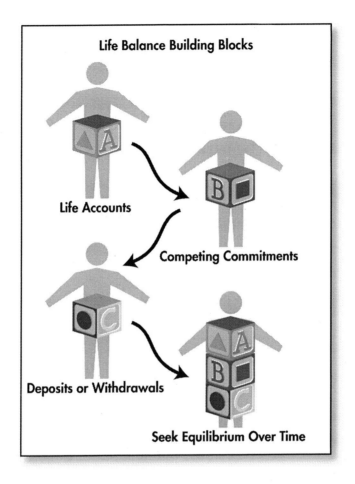

Figure 4.2.2

As we previously noted, Life Balance begins with the realization that each of us is comprised of four life accounts: mental, physical, emotional, and spiritual. These accounts, in turn, are constantly bombarded by competing commitments coming from a variety of sources. The competing commitments either add to (deposit) or subtract from (withdraw) the life accounts. Thus, over time, we must strive for equilibrium or balance in our life accounts in order to reach our full potential and derive the most from life.

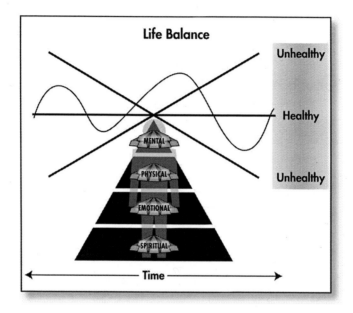

Figure 4.2.3

Now, for all you Type-A overachievers, you may draw the conclusion that maximizing deposits in all four life accounts enriches Life Balance--wrong! As Mama used to say, "Too much of a good thing spoils us."

If all your life accounts have an abundance of deposits, it could mean that you are coasting through life and not stretching to reach your full potential, just as an oversupply of withdrawals could indicate that you are at your limit necessitating rest and rejuvenation. Again, the objective is to seek equilibrium *over time* among the life accounts to *have it all as you define it!*

Why Seek Life Balance?

Perhaps the best way to answer this question is to tell you how others have responded to the same question. Some say reaching balance in their lives gives them an inner peace while others feel a sense of being in control. Other answers range from the ability to attain personal and professional goals to the preservation of their sanity!

Some people refer to Life Balance by posing this question: "Can I have it all?" Generally, they are referring to the ability to successfully perform numerous tasks associated with various life roles, such as parent, employee, volunteer, sibling, elder caregiver, church member, friend, and spouse. This view of Life Balance requires a personal clarification of *it* that fits within a person's discretionary time. Defining *it* will require prioritizing among competing commitments so you can have *it all* as you have defined *it*. Implicit in this definitional process is the understanding that you will redefine *it* many times as your life priorities change. The bottom line is this: you can have *it all* as you defined *it*; but you just cannot do *it all* at any one point in time. Thus, achieving Life Balance is a process that occurs over time.

Chapter 4.3

Having It All; Not Doing It All!

How Do You Achieve Life Balance?

"If you do not change your direction,
you will end up exactly where you are headed."
— Ancient Chinese Proverb

Here are some strategies to answer the question, "Life Balance--how do you achieve it?" First and foremost, you must recognize the need for and the benefit derived from Life Balance. If you desire to work toward improved Life Balance, then begin by envisioning what might constitute a balanced life for you. Visualize your life in the years ahead. Next, conduct a self-assessment of your four life accounts. Self--assessment requires an objective judgment and can conjure up some pretty uncomfortable feelings. How do you gain comfort when perform-ing self-reflection? Just do it--and often! In fact, seek input from others in your personal and professional life to gain insight, as well as validate your assessment. Once you have your vision of Life Balance and your self-assessment of how your life accounts currently measure up, highlight the gaps or areas that need change in order to gain equilibrium.

Fortune magazine described one corporate style as "the high-commitment model" which suggests, "your life should revolve around work and not much else" (Zimmerman 2-4). Of course, there is a price to pay for embracing the high-commitment model--giving up family vacations, Little League games, birthday parties, lunches and dinners, gardening, reading, movies, and most other pastimes. Dr. Alan Zimmerman, Certified Speaking Professional, acknowledges that in those high-commitment model corporate cultures, times are tough when it comes to Life Balance. He offers the following steps to begin the process to gain better balance in your life.

(1) Think about what you want out of life.

Your schedule, which is jam-packed with good things, may be allowing these good things to crowd out better things.

(2) Look at how your career is affecting your family.

Every work commitment has a consequence both now and in the future. Make sure that your consequences align with your family life.

(3) Refuse to be proud of your busyness.

We often get a sense of pride out of how busy our calendars become because it indicates how much in demand we are.

(4) Weigh the pros and cons of greater success.

Climbing the corporate ladder comes with more work and more stress. Is it worth it?

(5) Schedule your recreation.

    If you're a captive of your calendar, schedule your recreation because chances are, if it is not on your calendar, it will not get done. How many times have you said to friends, "we must get together," and how many times has it happened (Zimmerman, 2-4)?

    The next step in acquiring Life Balance is by far the hardest. This step requires *taking action* on the identified competing commitments that affect your Life Balance. The best advice for this step is to prioritize commitments, and then decide which commitments to eliminate, postpone, or reduce. It boils down to setting priorities and following through. During this step, involve those who are impacted by your decisions. Are you living your life by consciously chosen priorities, or are you going through life by default? But don't worry, if you don't get your Life Balance right the first time, you can always go back and realign. It bears repeating; attaining Life Balance is a process. It occurs over time. It is acceptable to acknowledge that for a specific period of time, certain accounts will be out-of-balance due to the nature of activities at that time in your life. Remember Figure 4.2.3.

    Set aside a specific time annually, like your birthday, to assess the status of your Life Balance. One last point that is worthy of emphasis: you will continue to *discover* your Life Balance; you will never really *attain* it. Strive to detect imbalance in your life and have strategies available to restore, even temporarily, Life Balance. Life Balance is like sailing. When you set sail, you furl the sails and adjust the rudder. You sit back, relax, and enjoy the journey. Then, the wind shifts or the current changes. It is time to alter the sails and maneuver the rudder. The journey becomes a series of constant checks on the course and making adjustments accordingly. Balancing your life requires the same kind of adjustments along the way.

NO SUBSTITUTES

Here is Vince's story about his own personal *imbalance*. As Vince reached his 50s, he realized he had four grown children, but he could hardly remember them growing up! As he worked to finish his education, move up the corporate ladder, and get ahead in life, he mistakenly minimized his involvement with his children. So Vince had this bright idea--he would make up for this with his grandchildren! Well, as much as he loves the grandchildren, and as much as he tries to spend time with them, it's just not the same as spending time with his own children. When the grandchildren do something special, his wife, Fran, will often say, "Oh, how this reminds me of when Vince, Rita, Lisa, or Jenny (their children) were growing up." No matter how hard he tries, Vince frequently cannot remember what it was like when their children did the same thing because he often was not there with them. So, if you have children and if you are not spending much time with them now, you too may be out-of-balance. Vince's experience is that you cannot make up for time lost with your children by adding more time with your grandchildren.

> Today, Vince's children tell him they feel he was always there when it mattered most. However, he still feels a tremendous loss of family experiences.

EVEN ICONS HAVE HEARTS

Here is Donna's story about *imbalance*. Working for an organization committed to executive training and development is a blessing. At least, that is what she always thought until she was caught between a tremendous opportunity and a once-in-a-lifetime event for her family. Her daughter, Amy, always liked to experience new and challenging activities. That is how she and her dad, Lloyd, became interested in the Soap Box Derby. Soap Box is a term applied to a kit car that is powered by gravity. With adult supervision, children, between the ages of 8 and 12, build these sleek, colorfully painted wooden and fiberglass cars with carefully balanced metal wheels, for the purpose of competitive gravity racing down large hills. The competition starts locally and builds through heats to the national level. Many community service clubs sponsor children for these competitions.

Donna was on a business trip when Amy captured the title, "City of Dayton, Ohio, Soap Box Derby Champion." However, she was able to share Amy's excitement during the celebrations that followed, including when Dayton's mayor decreed a day in Amy's honor and when she rode on a parade float with her purple unicorn soap box derby car.

Now, here comes the Life Balance challenge. Donna was scheduled to attend a competitively selected program at Harvard University in Boston for a month. Amy was to compete in the National Soap Box Derby in Akron, Ohio, during the same timeframe. Over the years, Donna's family had come to understand the challenges of a dual career household; however, no one could miss the look of disappointment on her daughter's face when she thought her mom might not be there. So, Donna went to the Harvard Program, and a week into the course, she built up her courage to meet with her advisor on the possibility of attending the national competition. She was pleasantly surprised to learn her advisor was familiar with the National Soap Box Derby. The advisor not only granted Donna's request, but set up time for her classmates to view the televised event!

Although this example turned out positively for all involved, it's important to remember that Life Balance is about choices and consequences. The challenge is learning to recognize the choices and consequences in advance and to make well-thought-out decisions.

Chapter 4.4

Having It All; Not Doing It All!

Show Me

"I skate to where the puck is going,

not to where it's been."

— *Wayne Gretsky*

According to the Center for Creative Leadership in Greensboro, North Carolina, when you are *balanced*, you are energized, on top of your game and poised for success. For Splendid Leaders, balance is a crucial issue--one that is rooted in personal choice. When a leader lacks balance, he or she is less productive in business and in life. Success and balance are two sides of the same coin. The better-balanced person is going to be the better-balanced leader.

Studies indicate that employees with Life Balance provide tangible and intangible benefits to business. Many companies are starting to pay attention to work policies and business strategies that embrace and enable Life Balance. Companies are recognizing that a satisfying personal life positively affects employee job performance (Hansen 2). Some of these policies include: flextime, telecommuting, on-site child and elder care, family-friendly leave, job sharing, in-house stores or services (post office, dry cleaners, auto maintenance, pharmacy, or dental), fitness centers, concierge services, and employee assistance programs. Businesses have learned that employees who are content with their Life Balance produce better products and services.

PRACTICING WHAT SHE PREACHES

Shirley M. Tilghman, President of Princeton University, is quick to recall the challenges of raising two children while pursuing her first career in molecular biology (Hechinger). Perhaps that is the reason she is such a strong advocate for creating a family-friendly workplace at the university. She offers the following five tips for supporting working parents:

1. Set a tone that says parents can care for their children and succeed at demanding jobs.
2. Give parents of young children longer time to compete for high-stakes jobs.
3. Automatically enroll parents in family-friendly programs to avert fears of asking to be enrolled.
4. Provide convenient, subsidized daycare.
5. Start a low-cost service that delivers babysitting and other help on short notice.

Ms. Tilghman practices what she preaches by extending the university tenure clock one year for every child you have while an assistant professor. This practice is applied in a gender-blind approach, extending it to both mothers and fathers. She noted that some family-friendly policies are not exercised by those who could benefit the most out of fear of being perceived as asking for a benefit. That is why Princeton University automatically extends the tenure clock. In a recent *Wall Street Journal* interview, she said: "The first lesson is no guilt. We have to allow women to say that it is fully legitimate to be at work; it is fully legitimate to be at home . . . and you shouldn't feel guilt when you're in either place. You do what you can do. It's about balance."

Pay-Offs

Of businesses studied where Life Balance is recognized and supported, the following *tangible* pay-offs were noted:

- ➤ Recruitment: When attracting the best and the brightest, especially relating to Generations X and Y, a lack of Life Balance is a deal breaker.

- ➤ Retention: Recruiting and developing employees is an expensive venture and directly impacts loyalty. A corporate commitment to Life Balance encourages employees to stay with a company, even when better financial offers could entice them away.

- ➤ Productivity: Workers who possess Life Balance supported by corporate policies are more productive workers. Workers attribute this increase in productivity to their desire to maximize their work contribution by only working on the most important tasks (no busy work) and by doing their work right the first time (no rework).

- ➤ Creativity: Employees working in product creation and marketing credited Life Balance with freeing their minds of distractions so that all their innovation is applied to the task at hand.

- ➤ Reduced Indirect Costs: Companies committed to Life Balance for their workforce were found to have less absenteeism and turnover.

- ➤ Customer Focus: Employees with Life Balance have their

priorities aligned such that their time at work is spent focused on customers' needs.

Although more difficult to measure but equally meaningful, companies who subscribe to Life Balance strategies for their workforce have observed the following *intangible* pay-offs:

- ➤ Harmony: Richer, more robust relationships are a natural outgrowth of Life Balance. These improved relationships are found on and off the job in many facets of activity.

- ➤ Enhanced Teamwork: Employees with Life Balance demonstrate increased collaboration and improved communication. The very nature of the discussions involved in gaining Life Balance reinforces a collaborative attitude that spills over into the work environment.

- ➤ Improved Attentiveness, Positive Attitude, and Confidence: These characteristics are present in a life-balanced work-force as a result of the knowledge gained from the self-reflection process.

- ➤ Pinpointing What Is Truly Important: Getting in touch with the four life accounts and the attendant competing commit-ments, inherently directs one to identify what is truly important, meaningful, and constructive in life. This behavior becomes habitual and is directly applicable to workflow.

Testimonies

Life Balance should be a concern for everyone. Consider Disney CEO, Michael Eisner, who refuses to work late if he has made a commitment to his children, or Columbia TriStar Motion Pictures Vice Chairman, Lucy Fisher, whose four-day schedule lets her dedicate Fridays to her family. Then, there is telecommunications mogul, John Malone, who works just five hours a day yet usually drives home for lunch, and Jill Barad, Mattel's hard-driving CEO and President, who ritualistically watches *ER* and *The X-Files* with her family (Hutchinson 17). An excerpt from a Price Waterhouse-Coopers annual statement notes the following: "We firmly believe that promoting work-life balance is a 'business critical' issue and not simply the 'right thing to do.'"

IT DOESN'T GET ANY BETTER THAN THIS!

Sometimes when individuals are striving to comprehend the concept of Life Balance, especially when they are in a fast-paced, ever-changing, pressure-packed, performance-driven culture, an attitude of skepticism or cynicism creeps in and threatens implementation of Life Balance. USAF General (Retired) William R. Looney, Commander, Air Education and Training Command, provided one of the best responses to this situation. In an interview and address to his workforce of thousands, he defined success not by the amount of money he makes, the rank he achieves, nor the position he holds, but by the balance in his professional and personal life. Being a talented, storytelling leader, he went on to share how he came to this philosophy.

He had received an appointment to the Air Force Academy and ultimately turned his flying dreams into reality. Interspersed between his many flying assignments, when he thought life just couldn't get any better, he was selected to attend the Armed Forces Staff College in Virginia. While attending this educational institution, Major Looney was among five other students who were requested to interview for a highly competitive position as a four star general's aide. During the interview, the general asked many thought-provoking questions, but perhaps the one that most caught Major Looney's attention was "Where do you intend to retire?" Now, as a major with ten years of service, this question struck Looney as strange and somewhat unexpected, because post-career planning was the last thing he was pondering. Major Looney responded to the question by saying that he planned to retire in Colorado Springs. A week after the interview, Major Looney was notified that he was selected for the assignment, and he moved to Germany to begin his new job.

Sometime later, while attending a social reception, Looney's wife, Marilyn, found the opportunity to remark to the general: "Bill and I have often wondered why you asked him about retirement when he was interviewing for the job as your aide." The general responded: "I asked Bill that question to see if he was thinking about other aspects of his life or solely focused on his military career. Knowing where you plan to retire indicates that you and your spouse have discussed what happens following the culmination of a career and that the military member is equally focused on a successful career, as well as a successful family life. Time is a preciously fleeting, finite commodity that once spent can never be recaptured. We need to think about how we spend that commodity by making family time a priority. The last thing you want is to have a very successful career at the expense of spending time with your family. Otherwise, when retirement arrives, there will be no family to share it." The general put his words into practice by balancing his professional and personal life and encouraging those he led to do the same.

In turn, General Looney adopted this same philosophy throughout his military career. He incorporated Life Balance in his mentoring and discussions about mission responsibilities. He communicated his commitment to Life Balance frequently and saw how it affected those he led by serving to enhance their performance. He clarified the implementation of Life Balance in the workplace by explaining that progress is made through the work of teams; very rarely is one person responsible for complex outcomes. Thus, when Life Balance is valued, it is easy for teams to meet their commitments. For example, when one of those personal priorities occurs, you step aside from your professional commitments and focus on the personal priority. This is made possible by supportive teammates who temporarily assume your work responsibilities while you attend to your personal priority. Then, when you return to resume your work responsibilities, it affords you the opportunity to fill in for your teammates when they experience similar personal priorities.

Now, here's the point of practicing Life Balance in the workplace: don't miss the piano recitals, anniversaries, birthdays, trips to the zoo, graduations, soccer games, track meets, scouting trips, and date nights with your spouse. Invest in your tomorrows today! General Looney found that this philosophy resonated with the workforce, making them more motivated, committed, and productive because their leader was committed to them and not solely to the mission. In his words, "True success requires a single focus, laser like approach to your career that accommodates both your professional and personal life."

Tips on Balance

With your newly acquired understanding of Life Balance, here are some tips to maintain that balance:

- <u>Learn to set limits and stick to them</u>. This prevents over commitment. Imagine tempting situations that could contribute to life imbalance and work up strategies or responses *in advance* of how you might handle them.

- <u>Take advantage of company policies that are Life Balance friendly</u>. These have been previously delineated earlier in this chapter.

- <u>Prioritize your many roles</u>. Deciding upon the relative priority of your roles as employee, spouse, parent, sibling, child, friend, volunteer, and so on, reduces psychological conflict manifested as guilt, pressure, anxiety, or stress. Protect each role; at work, shut off home intrusions and at home, turn off electronic ties to work.

- <u>Take care of yourself</u>. Manage your life accounts and competing commitments to engender joy and purpose into your life.

In conclusion, Life Balance, is about developing sensitivity to the four life accounts; assessing them with some regularity to recognize competing commitments and how they impact the accounts; then, applying the Life Balance process to seek equilibrium over time in order to achieve your full potential for a meaningful, fulfilling and enriching life. A final thought:

*"There is a choice you have to make in everything you do.
And, you must always keep in mind the choice you make, makes you!"*
— *Anonymous*

The Splendid Leader

Behavior Realities | Leadership Tenets | Essence of Leaders | Life Balance

Summary
The Four Pillars of Splendid Leadership

As we have stated, the *clout* of a leader's actions can dramatically affect and improve organizations. Many of us have lived through numerous organizational development concepts: Zero Defects, TheoryX/ Theory Y, Management by Objectives, Japanese Management Techniques, Quality Circles, Management by Walking Around, Just-in-Time, Total Quality, Integrated Product Teams, Strategic Thinking, Reengineering, Lean Thinking, Process Management, Strategic Intent, Transformation, Six Sigma and who knows what is coming next? Each of these concepts has the ability to positively improve organizations, and in many cases, they have had lasting impact. Furthermore, many of them are evolutionary, and they have successfully emphasized different elements of organizational or professional growth. However, as we think back over our 80 years of experiences with these different organizational development concepts, we see one enduring fundamental fact that is a constant among all of them. *If leaders do not get involved, the concept will not work!* Splendid Leaders are involved in changing organizations for the betterment of their employees and for the long-term viability of the organization itself.

At this point, we hope you have a complete understanding of the four pillars that support Splendid Leadership. We also hope you will look for these attributes in others as well as acquiring them for your own use. We believe leadership can be learned, so the best way to become a Splendid Leader is to be knowledgeable of the four pillars and to practice them in your personal and professional life.

As we looked back over our combined experiences, we asked ourselves, "How many Splendid Leaders did you know or work for?" Unfortunately, we could count them on one hand, and some people we interviewed spent their entire career without the opportunity to experience even one Splendid Leader. We are committed to doing all we can to right this wrong, and correct this inequity. Thus, we seek to arm as many people as possible with knowledge and understanding of the four pillars of Splendid Leadership in hopes that they will share them with others. If that happens, perhaps there is a greater possibility of seeing our vision of **"Splendid Leaders--EVERYWHERE!"** become a reality. We invite you to join us and spread the vision--in thought, word, and deed.

Works Cited

Back, Donna J., and Debra L. Haley. *Stop Juggling...Start Balancing!* Unpublished Work, 2007.

Barthelemy, Robert. *The Sky Is Not the Limit.* CRC, 1998.

Boyatzis, Richard, Daniel Goleman, and Annie McKee. *Primal Leadership.* Boston, MA: Harvard Business School Press, 2004.

Brizendine, Louann. "The Female Brain." *Dayton Daily News.* September 27, 2005.

Buntings, Madeline. *Willing Slaves.* UK: Harper Collins Publishers, 2004.

Cato, Steve. The Federal Executive Institute, Executive Development Course. Currently Distinguished Honorary Fellow. Antioch University, Seattle, WA, circa 1990.

Cherniss, Cary, and Daniel Goleman. *The Emotionally Intelligent Workplace: How to Select for, Measure, and Improve Emotional Intelligence in Individuals, Groups, and Organizations.* San Francisco, CA: Jossey-Bass Publishers, 2001.

Collins, James C., and Jerry I. Porras. "Building Your Company's Vision." *Harvard Business Review* (September--October 1996).

Fitz, Raymond, SM. Notes from personal interview, 2006.

Galinsky, Ellen. "Dual Centric--A New Concept of Work Life." Families and Work Institute, 2004.

Goleman, Daniel. "Leadership That Gets Results." *Harvard Business Review* (March-April 2000).

Goleman, Daniel. "What Makes a Leader?" *Harvard Business Review* (November-December 1998).

Graves, Laura M., Patricia J. Ohiott, and Marian N. Ruderman. "Managers Can Benefit from Personal Lives." *Leadership in Action*. Center for Creative Leadership. Hoboken, NJ: Jossey-Bass Publishers, January-February 2007.

Hansen, Randall S. "Is Your Life in Balance?" http://www.Quintessential Careers.com. 2006.

Hechinger, John. "The Tiger Roars." *The Wall Street Journal* (July 17, 2006).

Hunter, James C. *The Servant*. Roseville, CA: Prima Publishing, 1998.

Hutchinson, George. "Don't Just Survive--Thrive!" *Executive Focus* (May 2006).

Reina, Dennis S., and Michelle L. Reina. *Trust and Betrayal in the Workplace*. San Francisco, CA: Berrett-Koehler Publishers, 2006.

Russo, Vincent J. Unpublished notes. Executive Education Course by Professor Jack Weber. University of Virginia, 1998.

Sanborn, Mark. *You Don't Need a Title to be a Leader*. New York, NY: Doubleday Publishing, 2006.

Stroul, Neil A. "Coaching: A Conceptual Framework." Management & Training Innovations, Inc. Unpublished Work, 2001.

Thurston, Paul, et al. Air Force Institute of Technology Advisor for Several Thesis Topics, 2001-2002.

Zimmerman, Alan. "Become a Take Charge Champion: Perfecting Your Self-Management Techniques." The Institute for Management Studies, Columbus, OH, 2002.

Zimmerman, Alan. "Dr. Zimmerman's Tuesday Tip." Issue: #325. September 6, 2006.

Vincent J. Russo, PhD, is the President and CEO of Growing Splendid Leaders, LLC. In addition to his over 40 years of leadership and management experience, he has an academic background in leadership training from Harvard University's John F. Kennedy School of Government, the Brookings Institute, the University of Virginia's Darden School of Business, and the Federal Executive Institute. Vince has a long and distinguished history of structuring activities to help individuals and organizations grow their leadership skills. He is frequently requested by government, industry, and academic organizations to share his views on leadership.

Donna J. Back, CEC, is Chief Operating Officer and Chief Financial Officer of Growing Splendid Leaders, LLC. In addition to her nearly 40 years of leadership and management experience, she has an extensive academic background in executive development from University of Virginia, Penn State University, Carnegie Mellon University, Harvard University, the Federal Executive Institute, the Center for Creative Leadership, the Brookings Institute, and Georgetown University. She is a highly-sought national and local lecturer and speaker on a variety of topics including Mentoring, Work-Life Balance, Succession Planning, Intoxicating Leadership, Communication, Financial Management, and Process Improvement.